Learn To Use Your Modem in a Day

Richard A. Prendergast

and

David A. Brekke

Library of Congress Cataloging-in-Publication Data

Prendergast, Richard A.
   Learn to Use Your Modem in a day / Richard A. Prendergast and David A. Brekke.
      p.   cm.
   Includes index.
   ISBN 1-55622-445-1
   1. Modem.   I. Title.
   TK7887.8.M63P73   1995
   004.6'4--dc20   95-8551
                                                                       CIP

Copyright © 1995, Wordware Publishing, Inc.

All Rights Reserved   oo4.64
                              Pre

1506 Capital Avenue
Plano, Texas 75074

Printed in the United States of America

ISBN1-55622-445-1

10 9 8 7 6 5 4 3 2 1

9505

All inquiries for volume purchases of this book should be addressed to
Wordware Publishing, Inc., at the above address. Telephone inquiries may be
made by calling:

(214) 423-0090

Contents

Section 1
ABOUT THIS BOOK

INTRODUCTION

This book teaches you how to select, install, configure, and get the most from a modem. It should take you just a couple of hours to get to the point where you understand how modems operate and what to look for when purchasing one. Once you have chosen and obtained a modem, this book will assist you in installing and configuring it. This book contains exercises which are designed in such a way that you learn by actually doing. If you are like most people (yours truly included: we're called "tactile-kinesthetic learners") this is the most effective way for you to learn a new skill.

There is a good chance that you have several computer books sitting on your shelves at home or in the office, books that you have purchased with the best of intentions, but after a couple of chapters (or pages... *paragraphs?*) you found yourself in the program itself, poking around on your own and learning by discovery. Of all the methods of learning new software, this is my personal favorite. Although effective, it is unfortunately very inefficient.

If you just found yourself smiling and nodding, this book was written for you. It takes you through the many questions you need to consider when purchasing a modem and helps you understand just what it is you're buying.

ORGANIZATION

Following is a list of the sections in this book and a short preview of the contents of each.

HOW TO USE THIS BOOK

Start with page 1. Each section builds on the information discussed in the previous sections to one degree or another, so even if (like yours truly) you are somewhat random by nature, it would be best to approach this book in a sequential fashion. The first four sections prepare you to go out and find a modem that suits your needs. After that, it's all making the most of what you have. Even if you've already purchased a modem, the knowledge will help you later on. Obviously, a section that discusses something with which you are for some reason familiar is just begging to be skipped.

CONVENTIONS USED IN THIS BOOK

The following list defines several mouse and keyboard conventions used in this book. They are pretty common conventions, developed in the interest of brevity.

\<Enter>	Press the Enter key.
\<Esc>	Press the Escape key.
\<Down Arrow>\<Enter>	Press the Down Arrow key, release it, then press the Enter key.
\<Alt+F2>	Hold down the Alt key while pressing the F2 key.
\<Ctrl+Alt+Del>	Simultaneously press the Ctrl, Alt, and Del keys (not always a good idea).
Type this text	Type the boldfaced text.
Type this text \<Enter>	Type the text and press Enter.
Click	Click on a button, icon, etc.
Drag	Point to your selection, hold down the left mouse button, and pull it somewhere.

Section 2

WHAT IS A MODEM AND HOW DOES IT WORK?

INTRODUCTION TO COMPUTER SCIENCE

Most people are aware of the fact that computers process information in binary language. Even those who aren't would probably nod when informed of this. Right. Ones and zeros. Got it.

But what does that really mean? If computer A wants to communicate with computer B, A will have to send a bunch of ones and zeros to B, in some meaningful (to them) order, across some medium. This is self-evident. But how is it actually done?

We are not going to delve into the mysteries of how computers process information, store it, and retrieve it later. Let us concentrate instead on the communications part of the mystery. Taking things in order, we first must have something with which to connect the two machines. Perhaps a wire would do. Okay, we'll run a wire between the two computers.

Next, we need to send a bunch of ones and zeros across that wire. We'll worry about making the stream meaningful later. Luckily, we do not have to invent a way of doing this, since electricity hasn't changed much since the invention of the telegraph. First we electrify the wire. We'll pick a standard voltage of +5V DC. We'll make that equal to a "one." A "zero" will be represented by 0V DC, or ground. (We could just as easily have chosen the opposites, but since we're being totally arbitrary it just doesn't matter.)

So, by applying and removing voltage on the wire we have run between the two machines, we can send across a bunch of ones and zeros. That's easy. It looks like this:

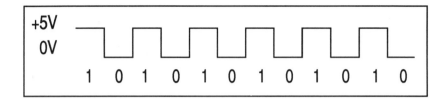

We did say something about making the stream meaningful, though. What if we want to send across fifteen ones in a row? Looks like we need to make the two machines agree on a standard length of time for transmission of each one and zero. For convenience let's refer to ones and zeros by the more generic term "bits." We can arbitrarily assume a standard transmission time for each bit of one second. So if machine A wants to send the stream "101101110100," it would take twelve seconds and look something like this:

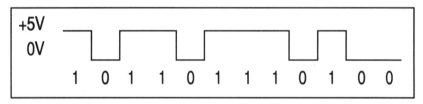

Since the machines have agreed on sending a new bit once per second, all machine B has to do is wait until A has begun transmission, wait another 1/2 second (to ensure that it isn't trying to read the value of the line while machine A is changing it), and start checking the voltage on the wire each second thereafter, as shown by the hash-marks in the following diagram:

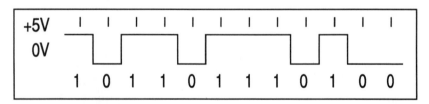

So now B knows what A is sending, doesn't it? Well, we sort of waved our hands through one very important part of the whole process. How does B know when A is ready to send bits? How does it know when A is finished sending?

It looks like we need another wire.

This new wire will hang out at 0V DC until A is ready to send data, then A will "take it high," or put +5V DC on it. When B notices that the new wire is now carrying 5 volts, it waits 1/2 second and starts reading bits. It continues to read a new bit every second until A takes the new wire low again (drops the voltage on the wire to 0V DC), then stops. Easy as pie.

Wait a minute, though. We really are only looking at half the problem. A can talk to B, but B is going to have to talk to A, if only to let A know B has received the data. No problem; we can add two more wires providing the same functions but in the opposite direction.

This is very inefficient use of copper, but it would work.

This actually gives us a lot more than two-way bit-dumping. It gives us secure communications. For example, if we want to be absolutely sure that B got the data that A sent, whole and in its entirety, the process *could* go like this:

- A sends a stream of bits, but keeps a copy for itself.
- B receives the stream, keeps a copy, and blasts it back to A.
- A receives the echoed stream, compares it to the original, sends a one if it matches and a zero if it does not. The zero is followed by a retransmission.
- B receives the next bit. If it is a one, B continues processing. If it is a zero, B dumps the saved stream and the two machines repeat the process.

Obviously this is all very cumbersome and would be painfully slow as well. There are better ways, as we shall discuss, but this should give you the general idea.

For example, we mentioned a very inefficient use of copper. Requiring four wires to implement bi-directional (sometimes called "full duplex") communication would not win an award from anyone except copper mine owners.

We *could* do it with two.

Say we chose, instead of +5V DC and 0V DC, +5V DC and -5V DC. Say we made the machines agree that once A took its line high, B would wait a predetermined amount of time and start reading. Knowing the amount of time B would wait, A would wait 1/2 second less and start transmitting. Communication in the other direction would work the same way. *Voila!* We just saved 50 percent on our copper bill. Unfortunately, we're greedy.

We *could* do it with one.

You probably already figured this one out. The above paragraph describes a technique that works just as well with one wire as with two, with a small exception. Whoever takes the line high becomes the transmitter, the other machine becomes the receiver. The only drawback is we can only operate in half-duplex mode, since both machines can't be manipulating the voltage on the same wire at the same time.

In reality there are many ways for machines to decide what is a one and what is a zero, and many more ways of sending said ones and zeros all over the place. In reality even an inexpensive modem can handle data transmission rates 19,200 times faster than our example. Computers are not very bright (one can only do so much with sequential processing of ones and zeros) but they are *incredibly* fast.

INTRODUCTION TO TELEPHONY

Assuming we have a workable means of transmitting bits across a wire between two machines, the next question could be, "What do we do if the machines are 6,452 miles apart?"

Well, let's see... we'll need four wires, that's 25,808 miles of copper... Perhaps we should investigate alternatives. There are fortunately people out there who have already run wire (or run fiberoptic cable, or built microwave towers) all over the world, and are more than willing to loan us the use of their facilities for a nominal fee. They are called long-distance carriers. Since we live in an acronym-happy world, we'll call them LDCs.

They have a network of interconnections that stretches from one end of the globe to the other. The only place they do NOT go is your house. (Strange thought, but true.) Back when all our phones were avatars of the BELL entity the distinction was not so great, but nowadays things are different. We have the aforementioned LDCs and we have Local Exchange Carriers, or LECs. They have networks that go out to everyone's house and connect them all to big (in some cases, very big) switches in centralized locations. The LDCs have high-capacity connections to these switches.

So, every time you call your Aunt Hortense in Twin Bridges, Montana, you dial (in most cases) a "1" followed by her phone number. The "1" informs the LEC switch that you are calling out of your "calling area." It checks the next three numbers, finds an area code, and hands the call off to the LDC switch. The area code tells the LDC switch where in the country to route your call. The next three digits are called the exchange (from whence we get "Local Exchange Carrier"), which tells the switch on the other end of the LDC's network which LEC switch should handle the call from there on out. The last four numbers point to your phone. All this hardware hangs around while you discuss virtual reality, peach pie recipes, and pork-belly futures. When you're done talking you hang up the phone and every piece of equipment notifies everybody up the line that the call has terminated. The resources that were allocated to handle your call are freed up and made ready for the next caller. You can connect to anyone, anywhere, with darned few exceptions, using the transmission facilities provided by your friendly telephone companies. What could be wrong with this wonderful arrangement?

Here is the problem: Their facilities are *not* based on ones and zeros. They are, after all, voice-transmission facilities. Yes, the LDCs have networks specifically designed for data transmission, but it is not really cost-effective for you to pay to have them run a line out to your house, unless of course you spend 80-90 percent of your time connected to various places around the world. The alternative is to find some way to translate between voice transmission and data transmission protocols.

WAIT! Your eyes just got glassy at the mention of protocols. Don't sweat it. They're not dangerous. You saw one earlier and didn't even notice. A protocol is just an agreement between two machines about things like how long bits should be, and what voltages are good for ones, etc. It's not rocket science, it just gets complicated trying to cover all the bases while the machines are compressing the data to shove more across in the same time, and sending simultaneously in 350 different frequencies to take advantage of available bandwidth, and stretching the bounds of space and time. Things like that make life complicated.

This looks like a fine segue into the next section. Enter the modem.

MODULATION/DEMODULATION

MODEM is short for MOdulator/DEModulator. Modulation is the conversion of digital bit streams into analog telemetry, suitable for transmission over phone lines. Demodulation is the reversal of that process.

Remembering the diagrams presented earlier, what was at the time obviously just fluctuations in the voltage on a line can also be considered a square wave of constant amplitude (peaks are always +5V DC, valleys are always 0V DC) and varying period or frequency (how long the signal stays high or low). So, the changes in amplitude tell us whether a one or a zero is present, and the changes in period/frequency give us the pattern of ones and zeros, the actual intelligence of the message.

As we discussed earlier, we specified 0V DC as "low" for simplicity, but really we would probably have made "low" the opposite of "high," or -5V DC. This would not really change the nature of the beast, just comb his fur a bit:

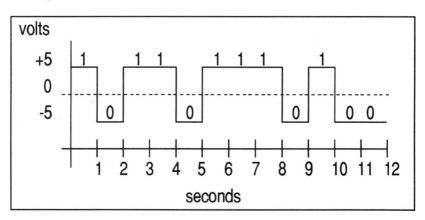

As you can see, nothing has changed. We're still sending the same message, "101101110100," it is still taking 12 seconds, and we're still representing ones and zeros by playing with the voltage on the line. The only difference is the specified value used to represent a zero. In fact, we could just as easily have chosen -5V DC to represent a one and +5V DC a zero. As long as both of our machines are configured the same way, it doesn't matter.

We had a nice neat method, didn't we? And then we had to go and muck it up with all these alternatives. As we shall see, this was unavoidable. The serial communications (we're not going to worry about parallel communications in this book) standard, "RS-232," actually specifies that a binary one is represented by negative voltage.

Five volts is a nice round number, but power supplies fluctuate, and we want to recognize a one whether we have two feet of copper connecting our machines or fifty (the maximum distance RS-232 signals can travel). Therefore, according to RS-232, any voltage from -3V DC to -15V DC will be acceptable as a one. If you get a seventy-five-foot cable to connect your two machines, you will get the infamous "unpredictable results." (Even tiny little copper wires have resistance, which means they don't like the idea of someone shoving a bunch of electrons down their throats. The longer the wire, the higher the resistance, so the trick is to pick a current (how many electrons you're shoving down the wire's throat) that, when it hits the resistance of the wire, results in a voltage between -3 and -15V DC. The only way to do this with any degree of accuracy is to limit the amount of resistance by limiting the length of the wire.)

Square waves are nice and neat and easily understandable, much like computers. They are either one value or another. Voice transmission facilities are not based on square waves, though. They are based on sine waves. Sine waves are not quite so neat. They look like this:

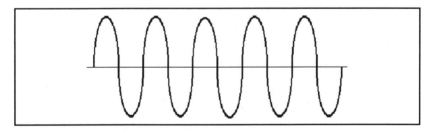

Voice transmission is achieved by manipulating an existing sine wave, or carrier. Obviously, converting a square wave into a sine wave for addition to an existing carrier is not a simple task, but luckily we don't care about that.

Suffice it to say that modems take a signal from a computer and encode it for transmission. Some examples of encoding techniques are "amplitude shift keying," "frequency shift keying," and "phase shift keying."

We've already discussed amplitude and frequency to a point, simply the height of the wave and how often it crosses the X-axis, respectively. Phase is just the point of the wave that crosses the Y-axis. In the following diagram, the top wave has a phase of 0 degrees. The second wave has a phase of 180 degrees. Their amplitudes and frequencies are the same. If transmitted together, these two waves would cancel each other out.

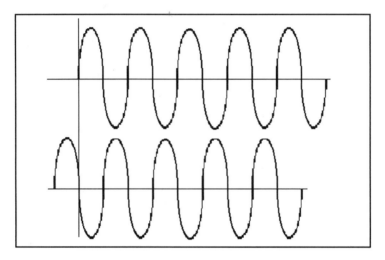

That is really all there is to it. A modem encodes a square-wave-oriented signal into a signal that can be added onto a carrier, and the other modem decodes it on the other end using the reverse of whichever technique was used to do the encoding.

Amplitude shift keying creates the new signal by manipulating the amplitude of the carrier. Frequency shift keying creates the signal by manipulating the frequency of the carrier, and phase shift keying manipulates the phase of the carrier.

THE RS-232 STANDARD IN-DEPTH

The RS-232 standard was introduced in August 1969 by the Electronic Industries Association to support connectivity between two particular types of equipment called Data Terminal Equipment (DTE), and Data

Communications Equipment (DCE). DTE usually means a computer, while DCE is a modem. The standard provides several different guidelines.

- Hardware configuration—This specifies the pin assignments and connector characteristics for the interface.
- Electrical configuration—This defines what signals shall be transmitted across the interface.
- Functional configuration—This specifies the function of each pin within the interface.

Hardware Configuration

The connectors that actually attach your computer to a peripheral device come in several different flavors. In the serial communications world, the de facto standard is a "D" type connector. The "D" type connector (more commonly called DB), actually describes the shape of the shell. The following figure illustrates two typical "D" shell connectors. The connector names are based on the number of pins/sockets within the connector. For example, a DB-25 connector has twenty-five pins or sockets, and a DB-9 connector has nine pins or sockets.

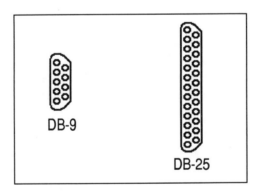

Pins refer to the "male" side of the connector. Sockets refer to the "female" side. Obviously, a pin plugs into a socket.

Electrical Configuration

The electrical signal characteristics specify that a voltage between -3V DC and -15V DC (with respect to a common ground), is interpreted as a binary 1. A signal that is between +3V DC and +15V DC is interpreted as a binary 0. Let's talk about "common ground" for a moment. We're not talking about facilitated group therapy. Common ground is simply what the two computers agree is 0V DC, or the complete lack of electrical potential difference between the two machines. Under rather bizarre circumstances, the two machines could be just dripping with electrical potential, but as long as there is no difference between them, they have a common ground. How this is implemented belongs under the next section.

Functional Configuration

Each pin/socket has a unique function. The RS-232 functional interface is broken down into two categories:

- Data
- Control

Data—Since they are called data lines, we can probably assume they are the lines that actually carry the data between machines. The following table describes the RS-232 data signals.

Pin/Socket	Mnemonic	Description
2	TD (BA)	Transmit data
3	RD (BB)	Receive data

Since this standard applies to all machines, we have a problem. Machine A and machine B are both going to be talking on pin 2 and listening on pin 3. This would not work well. We'll deal with how to get around that later.

Control—Control functions are used to manage the interface between two pieces of equipment. This basically means sending signals to the peer device indicating interface status and implementing flow control. The following table describes the RS-232 control signals.

Pin/Socket	Mnemonic	Description
1	GND (AA)	Protective ground
4	RTS (CA)	Request to send
5	CTS (CB)	Clear to send
6	DSR (CC)	Data set ready
7	SG (AB)	Signal ground
8	CD (CF)	Carrier detect

Pin/Socket	Mnemonic	Description
20	DTR (CD)	Data terminal ready
22	RI (CE)	Ring indicator
23	DSRS (CH)	Data signal rate selector

- Pin 1 is used to protect your hardware by using a common ground. This pin is generally not used in favor of pin 7.

- Pin 4 is used by the DTE device (i.e., computer) to inform the DCE device (i.e., modem) that the DTE device is ready to send data. The modem will respond with a signal on pin 5.

- Pin 5 is used by the DCE device (i.e., modem) to inform the DTE device (i.e., computer) that the modem is ready to receive data. Pins 4 and 5 are used for "hardware handshaking."

- Pin 6 is used by the DCE device (i.e., modem) to inform the DTE device (i.e., computer) that the modem is ready to communicate with the computer. This signal is another form of hardware handshaking and data flow control.

- Pin 7 is a common signal ground. This is mainly used by the hardware handshaking signals. It also provides the reference voltage of 0V DC, by which ones and zeros are measured.

- Pin 8 is used by the modem when the carrier signal is detected. This signal indicates that the local and remote modems have established a connection.

- Pin 20 is used by the computer when communications with the modem have been established. In short, the computer uses this pin to tell the modem it's ready to rock 'n' roll.

- Pin 22 is used when the modem detects when the ringer is utilized, usually when a call is detected.

- Pin 23 is used by the modem in determining the speed at which the remote modem is communicating.

In our previous (admittedly oversimplified) example, the wires on which we transmitted ones and zeros were the data lines. The lines on which we notified the other machine of our intention to send data were the control lines.

A real, honest-to-goodness RS-232 interface is a bit more complicated, but is nonetheless based on the same principles. It has two wires to handle transmission of data in two directions (pins 2 and 3). It has two more to handle the protocol of who gets to send when (pins 4 and 5).

That's pretty familiar. However, RS-232 also adds some things we did not. Pins 6 and 20 pair up to allow the devices to let each other know a connection has been established. Pins 1 and 7 provide common ground, which we frankly overlooked. The other three pins deal with modems doing that voodoo that they do: detect an incoming call, detect the presence of a carrier on which they can send data, and detect the speed with which the initiating modem is attempting to communicate. So excepting some minor details we were pretty close, wouldn't you say?

Cables

Since running wire between two machines and attaching connectors to the ends, paying careful attention to the colors on either side, being meticulous and thorough and all those things it is difficult indeed to be is not for everyone, cable come pre-made in various lengths, ready to plug in and go.

Remember we had a problem? Both machines were listening and talking on the same lines? Well, that's where the DTE/DCE distinction comes into play. The DCE device (modem) doesn't think of itself as something that transmits or receives data. It is only an intermediary. As such, it pairs up with its remote partner to handle the translation of those signals.

NULL Modem

What happens if the two computers are directly connected? We have no intermediary devices to translate, and DTE devices are supposed to talk to DCE devices. How do two DTEs talk?

A NULL modem cable solves this dilemma. This is a non-standard use of the RS-232 standard. This configuration tricks the DTE device into thinking that it is connected to a DCE device. This is accomplished by swapping wires. In the simplest configuration, pins 2 and 3 are swapped (so that A's transmit is B's receive, and vice versa) and pins 6 and 20 are swapped to allow each machine to let the other know it's ready to go. Pins 4 and 5 are fine as they are, 7 still provides ground, and the others are not used.

Simple, yet tricky. It fools the computer every time.

Handshaking

Handshaking is an understanding that exists between two devices reflecting the status and transmission of information over the interface. There are two types of handshaking: hardware and software. Both types of handshaking involve some sort of electrical signal exchanged between the devices.

Hardware—Hardware handshaking is a collection of electrical signals that provide functional characteristics of the interface. These functions are arranged into several widespread categories of data, control, timing, and ground.

Software—Software handshaking is a collection of data that constitutes a set of rules that must exist based on the type of interface. These rules or protocols are what is needed in order for two devices to communicate. Some examples of the most common protocols are XON/XOFF and ETX/ACK.

ASYNCHRONOUS VS SYNCHRONOUS COMMUNICATIONS

Asynchronous

Asynchronous communications, or start-stop transmission, is a character-oriented means of transmission. With this type of transmission, the receiving device has no clue when a character will be sent. Therefore, some overhead is needed in order to recognize that a character has been transmitted.

When a character is transmitted, extra information is added in order to distinguish between characters. This information, or framing, informs the receiving device when a character starts and stops. These are known as start and stop bits. In addition, another bit provides a simple form of error detection. This is known as the parity bit.

- The start bit is always located at the beginning of a frame, to notify the receiving device that a character has arrived.
- The stop bits are always at the end of each frame. There can exist several types of stop bits; one, one and a half, or two. There is

always at least one stop bit. A one and a half bit means that the length of a bit is greater than that of a normal bit.

- The parity bit is a method of checking whether the character transmission has been received correctly. The parity can be even, odd, none, space, or marked.

If even parity is used, the goal is to obtain an even number of bits. All the bits that make up the character are summed up. If this value is even, then the parity bit is set to zero, else it is of value 1. For example, if we want to send an "A" across to another machine, we would send a start bit, followed by the ASCII binary representation of "A," or 100001. There are two ones, so we would follow with a parity bit of zero.

Odd parity is like even parity, except the goal is to obtain an odd number of bits.

If no parity is used, then the parity value is ignored.

If space or zero parity is used, the parity bit exists always with a value of zero. This is used often when sending a 7-bit character to a device that is expecting to receive an 8-bit character.

There is a significant amount of overhead involved with asynchronous communications. An asynchronous transmission may take over 20 percent longer than a synchronous transmission.

Synchronous

Synchronous communication is a character-block-oriented means of transmission. The two devices actually synchronize to one another, and since the arrival times of character blocks are predictable, can transmit data at very high speeds. This method of communication is much more efficient.

The drawback of synchronous communications is that as the message transmitted gets longer, the two modems have a greater chance of drifting, or getting out-of-synch. If the timing or synch is lost, the entire message must be resent. These problems can be very costly.

We've solved the problem of transmitting data over voice-oriented lines; now let's move on to the software aspects of data communications: making two computers of different manufacture, era, operating system, location, and interface talk together.

Section 3

WHAT MAKES A GOOD MODEM GOOD?

If you're in the market for a modem, the best place to start shopping is your local public library. There you will find current and back issues of several different "bit-head" magazines, most of which regularly rate different pieces of equipment. Before you do this, though, several *caveats* are called for:

- These magazines are *not* consumer reports. They accept, indeed rely heavily on, the advertising money of the OEMs whose equipment they rate. If you read the same thing in two or more magazines, it becomes more reliable.

- Don't bother looking at anything over six to eight months old. The models may well have been replaced in that time, and the prices quoted are almost guaranteed to have dropped.

- Decide ahead of time what criteria are most important to you (features, warranty, technical support, price, etc.) and *then* read the article. This will help you make a decision based more on the facts presented and less on the author's bias.

These things being said, we can also assure you that you are unlikely to buy anything really *bad* if you act sensibly and don't purchase the latest addition to the albino slug venom family of modems, guaranteed MNP-11 compatible at speeds in excess of 250,000 baud, now available only through this special TV offer at only $19.95. Things move too fast in this industry for anything really awful to be around long, but gullibility is still punishable by being taken for a ride.

SOME THINGS TO LOOK FOR

While not all of these will be prominently featured in an article comparing modems, most if not all will be covered somewhere in the text. Most of these articles include a matrix showing the scores of all the modems being rated in each of the ratings categories.

- Adherence to Standards—Get used to seeing the name "Hayes." As IBM was to PCs, so Hayes is to modems.

- Error Correction—We'll cover some techniques later, but this is unlikely to be a deciding factor in your purchase, since all modems perform this function using one of just a few algorithms.

- Data Throughput—This is a biggie. Combining raw speed and compression and error handling efficiency, this is probably the best single measure of how well a modem does its thing.

ADHERENCE TO STANDARDS

When I bought my first PC (spring 1982), no two computer manufacturers used the same communications protocols, no one spoke anyone else's language, Microsoft had not yet taken over the earth, and once you bought a particular brand of anything, you were stuck. The bad old days ($800 for a dot matrix printer?) were not at all long ago. Soon after this particular episode, some people in the computer industry realized that picking a certain giant computer manufacturer's general design and logic and making "clones" based on that same design could make them a lot of money. (They've been doing it for so long now that the term "clone" is no longer in common usage.) Huge numbers of boxes with "100% IBM Compatible" stamped all over them were shipped. Most of these boxes actually had IBM-compatible machines inside. Thus were "de facto" standards born.

Jokes, too, were born of this.

"QUESTION: If (supercomputer manufacturer) Cray were to come out with a desktop computer that had 100 megabytes of RAM, sixteen processors operating at 200 million instructions per second (MIPS) each, and a 200 gigabyte hard drive, all for $450, what is the first question everyone would ask?"

"ANSWER: 'Is it IBM-compatible?'"

Standards have come a long way. Special Interest Groups (SIGs) made up of people from all over the world meet regularly to help move the development of intelligent standards along. Communications protocol standards are designed for Other Equipment Manufacturers (OEMs— other than computers, that is) to produce modulation/demodulation devices that are compatible with PCs and telephone lines. These standards include hardware, electrical, modulation and protocol specifications, most of which we have discussed previously. These latter include data compression and error correction algorithms, which also deserve a closer look.

In a nutshell, though, be sure that somewhere on the modem box it says "Hayes compatible."

ERROR CORRECTION

Earlier we learned about the parity bit used in the detection of errors. This is just an additional bit added to each byte during asynchronous transmission. This has its limitations: if a bit is reversed, the parity bit technique will discover it. If two bits are reversed, this technique cannot detect it.

1	1	0	0	1	1	0	1	Byte Stream Transmitted — Parity Is Odd
1	1	0	0	1	1	1	0	Two Opposite Bits Reversed — Parity Still Odd
1	1	0	0	0	0	0	1	Two Low Bits Reversed — Parity Still Odd
1	1	1	1	1	1	0	1	Two High Bits Reversed — Parity Still Odd

In the more general case, if an odd number of bits are reversed, the parity technique will catch it. If an even number are reversed, oh well.

Other more robust techniques include checksumming and CRC. These methods actually define another type of protocol. Another more sophisticated technique for transmission error control was invented by some folks working for an OEM. They called it the Microcom Networking Protocol (MNP). Initially, this communications protocol was proprietary. But because of its widespread acceptance it, like IBM's hardware design, became a *de facto* standard. MNP describes

10 protocol classes. The higher the class, the more efficient the protocol. The following table describes these classes:

Class	Description
1	An asynchronous half duplex protocol that is 70 percent efficient.
2	An asynchronous full duplex protocol that is 85 percent efficient.
3	A synchronous full duplex protocol that is 110 percent efficient. No frame information is used during transmission.
4	This protocol uses a dynamic packet transmission based on the errors detected and the quality of the medium. Efficiency is about 120 percent.
5	This protocol uses a real-time dynamic data compression based on the file type. Efficiency is about 200 percent.
6	This protocol utilizes the class 4 error-free transmission and the class 5 data compression. This protocol also provides the opportunity for the modems to agree on a transmission speed.
7	This is a sophisticated data compression protocol for 2400 bps modems. It provides an efficiency of around 300 percent, or a 3:1 compression ratio.
8	This adds the class 7 data compression to V.29 synchronous modems.
9	This adds the class 7 data compression to V.32 modems for transmission speeds of up to 38,800 bps over dial-up lines.
10	This is a protocol for modems attached to cellular phones. It is hard enough to send voice over cellular links, so the error correction in this protocol must be amazing. It is still proprietary.

DATA THROUGHPUT

In terms of communication transmission rates, the terms baud rate and BPS describe the rate of data transmission. The term baud rate is generally misused. It defines the length of a modulated signal divided into a second. This signal is not related to bit transfer.

On the other hand, bits per second (BPS) indicates the actual bits transferred in a second. This term more accurately describes the data transmission rate. Standards have been developed to provide a consistent means of specifying the speed of data transmission. These standards are based on the following characteristics: baud rate, BPS, modulation techniques, and transmission characteristics (i.e., asynchronous or synchronous). The following table describes some common data transmission standards:

Name	Baud Rate	BPS	Modulation	Transmission
V.21	300	300	FSK	Asynchronous
V.22	600	1200	DPSK	Asynchronous
V.22bis	600	2400	QAM	Asynchronous
V.27	1200	4800	DPSK	Synchronous
V.29	600	9600	QAM	Asynchronous
V.32	600	9600	QAM	Asynchronous
V.32bis	600	14,400	QAM	Asynchronous
V.33	600	14,400	QAM	Synchronous
V.34	600	28,800	QAM	Asynchronous
V.42	600	38,400	QAM	Asynchronous

You're probably wondering why the most common modulation technique is one we haven't mentioned previously. Quadrature Amplitude Modulation does not lend itself well to quick descriptions. In a nutshell, it uses black magic to somehow encode 2, 4, or 6 bits of information at once in a single frequency. Obviously this is going to send a lot more information in a lot less time than our single-bit transmission example from Section 2.

INTERNAL OR EXTERNAL?

In order for the modem to communicate with other modems, an interface must be established with your PC. This can be accomplished two different ways: with either an internal or an external modem.

An internal modem is installed inside your computer in an expansion slot. Because it is inside your computer, it receives power from the expansion bus. Internal modems are definitely more convenient (when they're working) than their external counterparts. They don't take up any space. They don't cause yet more wires to take over your office. However, installing them can cause the dreaded IRQ stress disorder (see Section 5). When for some reason they cease to work, there are no status lights to guide you in troubleshooting, and if they fail, you have to disassemble your computer to get at them.

An external modem requires an RS-232 cable connected to a serial interface card installed in the expansion bus of your computer. It requires an external power supply. The external modem does, however, have status lights, so one may observe the status of the modem at any time. It uses an RS-232 board already installed and configured (hopefully), so you don't have to worry about Section 5 (yet). Your modem User Manual will describe the lights it uses and what they tell you.

If an external modem breaks, you unplug it and bring it to your local modem repairman, without having to dissect your computer.

This is almost purely a matter of personal preference. Which is more important to you? Would you rather have convenience and a mess of cables running around your office, fill every plug within reach of your desk, and have cool lights to watch?

Or would you perhaps rather bite the bullet up front, find out about IRQs, poke around in the guts of your machine, have a neat office, room to plug in a lamp, risk having to take your machine apart again in the event of a problem, and have to find something to stare at other than the lights on your modem?

Like I said, purely personal preference.

SO, WHAT ARE YOU SAYING?

Obviously, standards are a big deal. If your modem adheres, you are unlikely to have a lot of problems talking to nearly any machine out there. Caution is advisable, especially when you see an advertisement for a modem made by a company of whom you've never heard, that supposedly out-performs anything else on the market, supports all the latest buzz words, and costs 70 percent of what all the others do.

We are not talking technical matters here; we're talking exercising good judgment and trying to buy quality at a fair price. Some people believe in buying quality even when it costs a lot more, feeling that it is always going to be worth it in the long run.

With computer peripherals, you may feel that everything you buy will be obsolete in two years (probably true) so you may as well buy cheap, since it doesn't necessarily have to last a long time. Bad idea, unless you own a computer repair business or are sweet on someone who does and want to spend a lot of time there. Longevity is not the issue in computers: initial quality, MTBF (Mean Time Between Failure), and technical support are the issues. Why do you think people routinely pay 30-60 percent more for genuine IBM® products and like it? Because they know that the chances are extremely high that they can plug it in and go without a hitch, and that if there is a hitch, IBM will bend over backwards to fix it, 24 hours a day, 365 days a year.

That, of course, is just one example. Since you're going to be doing research anyway, why not look up the ratings of computer equipment manufacturers according to their customer service departments? Some manufacturers have a reputation for treating their customers with kid gloves. Others have a reputation for treating them like the animal from which the kid gloves came.

We have a plan now. Library, research, tests, compatibility ratings, customer service, weighing all these things according to your own particular needs, and buying at a good price. That's covered. Let's get on to the software.

Section 4

WHAT KIND OF SOFTWARE DO I NEED?

So far we've looked at the basics of computer communications, a simple example of direct-connection methodology, a minor smattering of telephony to illustrate the need for something other than direct-connection communications, modems and how they fulfill that need, and the steps necessary to find a good one that fits your budget. And you're still not satisfied.

That's understandable, since we've only looked at one side of the fundamental problem. All of the items in the paragraph above have dealt with the hardware we need to make our machines talk to each other over long distances. This is necessary, but not sufficient. A computer is an expensive paperweight until someone puts some software on it that tells it what to do.

Interestingly enough, what we now want it to do is much less than it is used to doing. Got that? If you want to do something really simple, like write letters to friends on your computer, you load a word processor. Ever consider what goes into writing a word processor? The word processor has a screen driver to display your work, and its own command language that allows you to do things like searches, replaces, insertions of various things no one ever put on a typewriter, etc. It also has format control, various tools for spelling, pagination, grammar, and automatic table of contents generation. It has a DOS file system interface that allows you to save your work and an automatic save utility that does it when you forget. That's a lot of software.

To communicate with a host computer, we still need a screen driver to see what we're doing. We need a DOS file system interface in case we want to download or upload files. ("Download" always means from host to client machine. "Upload" always means from client to host. Clients initiate connections with hosts.) Other than that, we need some means of taking the characters we type and having them show up on the host machine as though we were sitting at the host machine's keyboard. That, of course, is a bare-bones outlook on what we need, not a description of what we want.

What DO we want? How do we know when we're getting it? Presented here are a summary of communications software features and some examples of products. While we are not going to plug a particular communications software package, there are packages out there that have become famous over the years for quality and reliability, so they deserve a mention here and there.

FILE TRANSFER PROTOCOLS

This is a very critical feature. Specialized file transfer protocols allow file transfers between computers while monitoring errors that may be introduced during the transfer. Let's take a look at some of the most common protocols:

Kermit

Yes, this was named after the famous frog. It started out in the academic world, having been developed by Frank DaCruz and Bill Catchings at Columbia University. It is still extremely popular. The complete Kermit manual is available by writing to: Kermit Distribution, Columbia University Center for Computing Activities, 612 West 115th Street, NY, NY 10025.

Xmodem

This file transfer protocol was developed in the mid-1970s by Ward Christensen and placed in the public domain. It was intended for transferring files over 300 and 1200 bps modems connecting CP/M machines. If you were surprised to hear that Paul McCartney was in a band before Wings, you probably have never heard of CP/M. It was one of the very few competitors DOS had before Microsoft conquered the earth. In spite of this, Xmodem's public domain status and general ease of use kept it popular for a very long time.

Ymodem

There are several flavors of Ymodem. The basic version was written as an extension to Xmodem to get around some of the former's shortcomings. It was designed by Chuck Forsberg to increase the block size from 128 to 1024 bytes and enable the sending of information about the file along with the file itself. One of the variants, YmodemG, sends the whole file before performing any error-checking. If an error is found, the entire file needs to be resent. This works very well in the world of modems with hardware-based error detection.

Zmodem

This is the leading protocol for high-speed file transfers over dial-up lines. It has 32-bit CRC, server functions, batch mode, and the ability to pick up where it left off if it gets unplugged in the middle of a transfer. Zmodem was funded by Telebit, designed by our old friend Chuck Forsberg, and placed in the public domain.

CompuServe B

As the name suggests, this protocol is for exchanging files with the access provider CompuServe.

ASCII

We already talked about the ASCII character set. This is essentially a simple file transfer protocol, too. It relies on the hardware or the transport layer to perform error-checking.

TERMINAL EMULATION

Terminal emulation allows your Intel 80X86-based computer to communicate with systems that know nothing of such beasties. Your computer's (software's) ability to convince the remote system that it is actually a Digital Equipment Corporation Video Terminal, or an IBM 3270, is a major factor in your ability to communicate with a wide variety of platforms. Some common terminal emulators include VT100, VT220, VT300, WYSE 100, TVI 920, IBM 3270, and ANSI.

The VT100 has been around since video terminals were new-fangled things that would never replace the good-old teletype. The 220 and 300 were updated versions of the same. DEC now has 21" graphics-based terminals designated VT1300 and above. When in doubt, choose VT100. Nearly everybody supports it.

One would think that IBM's 3270 or ANSI terminal definitions would be the most widely used, but it just isn't the case. The 3270 terminal is used exclusively with IBM mainframes, and although ANSI (American National Standards Institute) is by definition the standard, no one has caught up to the VT100 in sheer volume of support.

SCRIPTING LANGUAGE

We're always trying to save keystrokes, so early on someone came up with the idea that one could turn on a recording program, issue a command that got issued with great frequency, turn off the recording program, and save a whole bunch of time next time. That's called defining a macro, and it was great for simple commands of limited scope that never varied. Several months went by, everything changed, and macros just weren't enough anymore. The next step: the scripting language.

A scripting language allows you to create a program that automatically issues the keystrokes necessary to complete a desired task. Because it is actually a program and not just a recorded procedure, it can be run 100 times and never issue the same exact sequence of keystrokes.

This is the real power of your software. If the software you buy is anything like the copy of PROCOMM PLUS 2.0 for Windows sitting on my disk, the manuals tell the whole story. The user manual is 3/4" thick and covers everything pretty completely. The Windows Aspect Script Language manual is twice as thick. Remember, a scripting language is just that: a new language for you to learn. Many people never get to the point where they need the power of a scripting language. Those who go to the trouble of learning it and using it wonder how they got along without it.

A simple example: you walk by your machine, click on the PRODIGY button, and go to the kitchen for a quick chocolate-covered banana. Meanwhile, your script logs on to PRODIGY, gives your password, checks your e-mail, downloads the files it finds there to your machine's incoming messages directory, uploads any pending messages you had written and not sent, sends them, checks your designated SIG for action, scans some news stories using keywords you gave it, looks over the latest Dow Jones quotes, notes the prices of some of your favorite stocks, looks to see if ID Games has gone public yet, grabs all the data it uncovers, downloads it to the appropriate places on your disk, logs off, and exits. Not only was that much easier than sitting there and typing all that in by hand, but because it was done with a machine's efficiency, you probably saved 50 percent in access costs and had time for a great chocolate-covered banana in the bargain. Now THAT's power.

BULLETIN BOARD SERVICES

BBS features (this is also called host mode) allow your computer system to actually behave like a bulletin board system. You can set up user accounts and transfer e-mail among users and host files for file transfers. Not many people do this, although the number of privately-run BBSs out there is staggering. Most are free-access and contain the numbers of other BBSs. Once you start looking, you can go on an odyssey worthy of a Michener novel. If this is something you want to do in a big way, you'll need a very capable machine, a blazingly fast modem, and preferably several lines on a rotary to offer access to more than one user at a time. So as not to drive those users crazy waiting for a return, you'll have to find another operating system. There are several versions of PC UNIX out there, which seems to be the operating system (OS) of choice for large servers. This can get complicated very quickly, but if all you want to do is share data among some friends, the right software will make it pretty easy.

FLEXIBLE SETUP

Flexible setup provides you the ability to custom-tailor how your software will interface with your hardware. Examples include modem prefix and postfix commands, modem initialization strings, computer interrupt configurations, software file transfer directory locations, and keyboard mapping.

CONTEXT-SENSITIVE HELP

Context-sensitive help will give you immediate answers, examples, and suggestions about any questions that arise while using the software package. Wherever you are in the hierarchy of the program, context-sensitive help will offer you help based on your current position, rather than offering you a table of contents from which to begin your (often arduous) search.

PHONE DIRECTORIES

Phone directories maintain lists of your most frequently called numbers. You can set up directories for different areas, like a business directory, a home directory, an investment directory, even one for your kids, possibly allowing for statistics on how often and how long you call a particular number and a password protecting you from any outside influence.

SECURITY

The ability to password-protect your script files, require passwords to gain entry into your system, and provide a dial-back feature with your BBS option to prevent strangers from exploring your computer are just a few of the possibilities. Once you open up the world, the world can come to you, too.

SOME EXAMPLES

Some of the more popular communications software packages include Carbon Copy, Crosstalk, PROCOMM PLUS, Qmodem, Relay Gold, Smartcom III, and pcANYWHERE. The recommendations in Section 3 about looking for a good modem apply here as well: decide what you need before you start looking at magazine comparisons. Pay special attention to the dates in these cases. Often a release will come out that just doesn't quite cut it, a review will be published that rips the software in question to pieces, and the next release will fix everything the reviewer lambasted.

Be sure you're comparing the latest and greatest of each company's offerings. For example, PROCOMM has been around since triple-digit baud rates and has gained quite a reputation for being a good, solid program that got the job done without a lot of bells and whistles. PROCOMM PLUS for Windows version 1.0 came out, and although the reviewers were not in most cases overtly hostile, the word was that you were better off running the DOS version. When version 2.0 came out, the bandwagon's axles broke from the stress of all those people jumping on it. It's a great program.

If you want to ease into this, MS Windows comes with a Terminal program that provides some of the basic capabilities we've discussed in this section. Terminal allows you to configure your modem interface, modem prefix, and postfix commands, choose between a couple of terminal emulations, and transfer files using Xmodem or Kermit. You can use this package to get started and gradually build an idea of what you need before shelling out the money on a major communications software package.

Next, we'll take a look at interrupts, why they're important, why they are cruel and evil harbingers of doom, and what you can do to either avoid them or tame their beastly hides.

Section 5

STOP INTERRUPTING ME!

GETTING YOUR MODEM INSTALLED WITHOUT SUBSEQUENTLY REQUIRING THERAPY

This is easy: buy an external modem. Okay, we said that it was a matter of personal choice and all, but one of the factors entering into that choice is your willingness to chance mental breakdown. When you purchase an external modem, you tie up a serial line that you might well want for something else, so that may not be a good thing for you.

However, the good part about purchasing an external modem is that it ties up one of your serial ports.

How's that again?

Well, the good part is not really that it ties up the port, but that it uses an existing port, which the manufacturer already had to set up to talk with the CPU. This makes installation a very simple task indeed: plug it in, configure it, and use it.

An internal modem naturally leaves all your serial lines free. This is a good thing. The bad thing is that it leaves all your serial lines free. Sensing a pattern here? If you don't use an existing, configured port, you have to take whatever steps are necessary to make it talk to the CPU yourself. Thus the risk of mental breakdown. This is certainly doable by anyone willing to put in the time to learn the steps and then execute these steps in the proper order, exercising the proper care.

"The thing ya gotta ask yourself, punk, is 'Do I feel lucky?'"

IRQ STRESS DISORDER

Every device that you plug into your computer needs some way to talk to the CPU. That's called a bus. Not the derivative of "omnibus" that we all hate to ride on, but a sort of switchboard inside the computer that allows the CPU to converse with any external devices with which it needs to converse.

The architecture is there, and the CPU is more than willing to do its utmost to meet everyone's needs. Of course, in order for you to converse with it, you must first let it know that you have something to say. That's where the Interrupt ReQuest channel (IRQ) comes in.

There are several IRQs available for use. They are represented by wires on the motherboard and in the slot connectors. (If you've installed an internal modem, or any other internal device, for that matter, you know what we mean.) When a particular IRQ is *invoked*, a special routine called *interrupt control software* takes over the system, saves everything the CPU was doing when it was interrupted, and directs the system to the *interrupt vector table*.

(Okay, slow down, take a deep breath. It's not as bad as it sounds. It's just a means of looking up, for each IRQ, the location in memory of the program that invoked the interrupt. Say you carry a pager. You're tooling along, minding your own business, and it goes off. That's invoking an interrupt. You look at the little display and see a phone number. The display is the equivalent of the interrupt vector table. The phone number is the entry in that table that tells you where to go to connect with the sender of the interrupt. The analogy breaks down in several places, but you get the idea.)

Once the CPU has finished serving the needs of the modem, the interrupt control software goes out and grabs everything the CPU was doing before it was so rudely interrupted and reloads it. The CPU continues on as before.

Think of it as call waiting. You're discussing orange juice futures and vacuum cleaner bags with your Aunt Hortense in Twin Bridges, Montana, and a call comes in. You hear the click (IRQ), you enter a special routine whose first instruction is called *apologize and ask Aunt Hortense to wait for your return* (interrupt control software), stick everything you were talking about in the back of your head (save contextual information from current program) and hit the button to connect you with the other party (go to the interrupt vector table, which in this case only has one entry). You deal with them, try to remember what you and Aunt Hortense were discussing (reload contextual information from before the IRQ), and hit the button again (return to previous program).

So, to get your peripheral device to talk to your CPU, you simply need to choose an unused IRQ, let the device know which IRQ to use when it has something to say, and let the system know which device drivers to go to when that IRQ is invoked.

That's all there is to it. In theory. As with most things, in practice it can get a bit messy.

THE PRACTICE

This really is doable. My dad has been a professional mechanical engineer for about 40 years, can calculate with a slide rule faster than I can with an HP-12C, and recently (ten days before Christmas, of course) bought himself a modem. His children were going to get him one (an external one—we didn't want to give him IRQ stress disorder), a fast one, with all the extras, but he went out and bought an internal modem and installed it himself. Apparently it took most of a day.

I have not seen him since he did this, and he was unable to express the feelings he had about IRQs over the phone (also, my mother was on the line, and he may not have felt comfortable using the kind of language one needs to discuss IRQs with her present). The thing is, this is a very intelligent man, used to analyzing systems, good with his hands, extremely thorough and meticulous. Why did IRQ stress disorder nearly take his life?

Lack of information. Just you try to find something useful about IRQs in the DOS manuals, or the Windows manuals, or the on-line help facilities for either of them. Not a thing. If you dig really hard, you might find a definition of the acronym somewhere.

So, say you already went out and bought yourself an internal modem, or you hate the clutter of wires and lack of electrical outlets that go along with external devices. What can you do to avoid this dread disease?

Step number one: read everything you can get your hands on that tells you anything about IRQs.

Step number two: find out all you can about the way IRQs are set up on your particular system.

Step number three: read the manual that came with your device (from here on out we'll assume it's a modem, but it doesn't have to be) and find out what IRQ it was set to use at the factory.

Step number four: once you have found the place where the manufacturer tells you how the modem was configured by default, search that section for instructions on how to change the configuration.

Step number five: using your new-found knowledge, choose an IRQ that your modem supports and that your system isn't already using, configure your modem to use that IRQ, and tell your system that it is now used by a modem.

Let's take these steps one at a time and look at them a bit more deeply.

Read Everything

Unfortunately, there is not a lot of information about IRQs out there meant for the casual reader. I have a 1,300-page tome about PC repair that devotes five of those pages to IRQs. If you've read this far without skipping to Section 6, you probably have a pretty good idea what's going on and can proceed to the next step.

Study Your System

If you have DOS 6.2 or later, you have a utility called "MSD," which stands for Microsoft Diagnostics. It is capable of going out, examining your system, and determining what IRQs are used by what devices. If you are running an earlier version of DOS, you would be well-advised to upgrade. It doesn't cost that much, and this utility alone is worth the money.

There are 16 IRQs available in 80x86- and Pentium-class machines. They are numbered 0 through 15, described in the following table:

0	Timer
1	Keyboard
2	Used to access IRQs 8-15
3	Serial Port 2
4	Serial Port 1
5	Parallel Port 2
6	Floppy Drive Controller
7	Parallel Port 1
8	Real-time Clock
9	Available as IRQ 2
10	Available
11	Available
12	Mouse
13	Math Coprocessor
14	Hard Drive Controller
15	Available

Now that we've described the interrupts using a table, let's describe the table. The original PC/XTs (for those of you that can remember that far back, they were 8-bit machines that ran at 4.77 MHz, or just slightly faster than glaciers), being 8-bit machines, had only 8 interrupts.

The advent of the 16-bit AT-class machine, otherwise known as the 80286, meant more addressable space and twice as many interrupts, thanks to the addition of another Intel 8259A controller.

Problem: we have another chip and 8 more interrupts, but no way to get to the extra interrupts; don't ask why. This was solved by taking IRQ 2 and wiring IRQs 8-15 through it using a technique called "cascading." Now we can get to all our IRQs, but we used one for overhead, so we really only have access to 15 of them. Also, IRQ 2 is used by a lot of devices, so just yanking it out and using it for overhead is not going to work, so IRQ 9 was wired through to IRQ 2.

What the heck am I talking about?

Remember, Interrupt ReQuest channels are wired to slots on the motherboard. IRQ 9 was wired to the slot that IRQ 2 used to service, making it available to 8-bit adapters as IRQ 2 and providing some compatibility to older peripherals.

This is not a big problem, many years and several generations of processors later, but the architecture remains.

In essence, you can just remember that not all IRQs are available. On most machines, you can safely assign at least a couple of the following IRQs: 2, 3, 5, 7, 10, 11, and 15. Only you and your computer manufacturer know for sure.

Determine Your Modem's Factory Settings

This is definitely one of the things to consider when choosing a modem: how good is their documentation? How easy is it for you to find out what the factory default IRQ is? How easy is it to change it? Does the modem use DIP switches or jumpers or both? If your choice of modem is already made and you have found it to be lacking in this area, use the 800-number (let's hope you bought from a company that has one) and get technical support on the line. They can tell you what your modem was set to when it left the factory and lead you through changing it.

Determine How to Change Them

This is not a case of issuing a command to some software and watching the magic happen. Most if not all internal devices are hardware-configured where IRQs and other protocol-level parameters are concerned. This means that if you want to change the factory setting, you need to identify the DIP switches or jumpers involved and move them in some predetermined way to get the desired result.

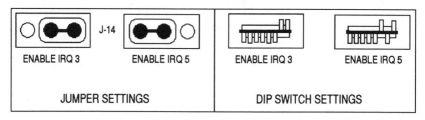

The above example is of course just that, an example. There are several bazillion ways to build IC boards, and every one of them is used by someone. Your manual should tell you which jumper or switch set changes what value and hopefully will even include a diagram telling you where on the board to find said jumper or switch.

Jumpers are just little plastic things that connect two posts on an IC board. The posts are usually about the size of a tack and come grouped in threes. If you want IRQ 3, you put the jumper across the right two posts, connecting them. For IRQ 5, you put it across the left two posts.

DIP switches (DIP stands for Dual Inline Package—don't ask why) are easy to deal with if you watch out for the one major "gotcha" associated with them. As you can see in the diagram, they're just tiny little toggle switches in a row. They control electrical flow to one or more chips, thus resulting in different configurations depending upon their state.

This is basically binary, with up being 1 and down being 0, so with eight switches, there are 256 possible configurations. Luckily, your documentation will usually say things like "put switch D up" which is pretty easy to understand.

The gotcha comes in trying to figure out which way is "up." This sounds facetious, but these switch banks can appear in any orientation you can think of, and which way is "up" is not always obvious.

Choose an IRQ and Use It

Once you have determined what IRQs your system has open and figured out what IRQs your modem supports, you find a place of intersection and say, "That is the IRQ for me!" You get out your needle-nosed pliers and move whatever jumpers (or get the toothpick out of your Swiss army knife and flip whatever DIP switches) need to be moved (or flipped) and with extreme care plug your modem into an open slot on your motherboard.

You probably received some software with your modem, mostly the drivers needed by the system to talk the modem's particular brand of binary. The installation program for these drivers will ask you for the interrupt you wish the device to use if it cannot go to the modem and ask how it's set. If the modem can't tell it what IRQ you set, you can.

If the installation program is primitive and assumes factory defaults, you will have to run a separate setup program, which will also be included with your modem software. These are usually very easy to understand and have on-line help facilities if you get stuck.

Also, don't forget that 800-number. That's what they're there for. Just don't call until you've read the documentation, looked at the situation, and tried to figure it out. People who work at help desks hear from too many people who didn't bother to read anything, try anything, or look at anything before calling.

Once you've gotten past the installation of your internal modem, you will quite justifiably feel that you can accomplish anything. The computer loses much of its mystique once you've spent some time poking around in its innards, and with familiarity comes a lessening of apprehension.

Need more memory? You can install it yourself. Want to add a hard drive? Piece of cake. Feel like adding some cache? A sound card? 32-bit graphics accelerator with 2 meg on-board? Child's play. You've installed an internal modem.

Okay, you have a modem. The CPU knows you have a modem. You have settled on a means of letting the CPU know your modem has something to say. You have some data communications software. Now what?

Well, you've configured it to talk to your machine, now you have to configure it to talk to other modems.

Section 6
WHAT DOES 19200:N:8:1 MEAN?

A BREAKDOWN OF MODEM CONFIGURATION

Now you have chosen a modem and plugged it in and purchased software and loaded it. Your software comes up and starts asking you how it should configure the connection you've given it. Huh? What baud rate? How many start/stop bits? What parity will you use? What the heck is mark parity? Is that anything like subatomic particles? You are dazed and confused. Luckily, the software provides defaults for all of these, so you allow it to load all defaults and congratulate yourself on your ingenuity. Then disaster strikes.

You make your first connection to a BBS that doesn't reside at the company from which you obtained your software and you get gibberish. Go figure. What are you going to do now? What do all these numbers mean, and what good are defaults if they don't work?

We've already discussed the "19200" part of the equation. It is often referred to as baud rate, really means bits per second, and is a function of data transfer rate and compression combined. Modems are getting pretty sophisticated these days and run some wild compression algorithms and far-out multiple-band simultaneous transmission methods, so saying that a modem transmits at 19200 baud doesn't really mean much. (Actually, it probably means that the modem is transmitting at 2400 baud, using four frequencies to transmit four bits at once, and compressing the four streams at a 2:1 ratio. But that's not important now.)

No matter how sophisticated the compression and multiple-frequency transmission algorithms get, pretty much all modems nowadays perform a function called "auto-stepdown" when connecting to a modem running at a lower speed (which of course translates to less sophisticated algorithms). Auto-stepdown means that if a modem running at 38400 baud connects to a modem running 9600 baud, it backs off the fancy stuff until the two modems can agree on a set of algorithms they both can handle. (That's what you're hearing when two modems trade high-pitched whines for a few seconds before everything gets quiet and you connect up. They're trading information about how they like to talk until they hit upon something that makes them both happy.) Because of this function, it is unlikely your gibberish is a result of a speed mismatch.

Let's assume both ends of the connection are operating at 19200 bps for now, they're using the same compression and transmission algorithms, the line is clean, and everything looks normal (as far as looking helps you determine anything where modems are concerned). In order to get a handle on the various possibilities that could account for your problems, perhaps we should take a look at modem functions. After all, if you want to figure out why something doesn't work, it helps to know what it's supposed to do. The basic functions of a modem are dialing, answering, and disconnecting.

Dialing

In order to dial a number and establish a connection with a remote computer, your modem must be configured properly. What is the criterion by which "proper" configuration is decided? Whatever the configuration is on the host (answering) side.

Your (dialing) modem must know the following things:

- What number to dial
- Whether to use tone or pulse dialing
- How long to wait for a carrier
- What to do when a carrier is detected
- At what speed the modems will converse
- What computer/terminal interface (i.e., Data Terminal Ready) to use
- What type of data compression to use
- Whether it should echo the command controls to your communications software
- What type of data flow control to use between the modem and your computer

If the first parameter is not correct, you get terribly embarrassed and damage some poor soul's hearing with the modem's carrier tone. If number two or number three is not correct, you get all or nothing; it either works or it doesn't. If number five is incorrect, you rely on your modem's ability to detect the discrepancy and step down to a slower bps-rate. If any of the others are not correct, you will in all probability get gibberish.

Admittedly, that was not a very strong statement. Not at all like "In this case you will receive all characters offset by ASCII 0X48." People generally think that with computers things are very black-and-white, on-or-off, working-fine-or-pouring-smoke-into-the-room. This is unfortunately not the case. With computers in general, and *especially with communications between them*, configuration and troubleshooting is more an art than a science.

Answering

If you wish to act as a host, you must configure your modem to answer a call from another modem. Your (answering) modem must know the following things:

- Whether it should answer the phone
- On what ring the modem should go "off hook"
- How long to wait for a carrier signal
- What controls should be returned to your communications software
- What type of data flow control to use between the modem and your computer

Once you have configured your modem with this base set of characteristics, it will work out the rest of the configuration information with the dialing modem through the process described earlier. Once this has occurred, all that remains is the transfer of data.

Disconnecting

Surprisingly, there is more to disconnecting than hanging up the phone. First a modem must be commanded to disconnect by its controlling software. Second, it must send a signal to the other modem telling it to hang up, too. If this does not happen, obviously we would hope the controlling software would realize it and tell its modem to hang up, but there would be a delay. Delays cost money.

Also, it is just not good design to leave loose ends lying around like that. Just as we (being good, considerate people) are sensitive to the feelings of the party on the other end and don't just hang up when we're done speaking, our modems send the equivalent of a "I'm hanging up now, so you should too."

Each of the modems then drops its respective carrier, and the connection goes away. They must then re-initialize and wait for the next task to come down from the controlling software.

So what happens when this clean, sweet process breaks down? One of three things:

- You cannot make a connection.
- You make a connection which immediately goes away.
- You make a connection and get gibberish.

You Cannot Make a Connection

If the parameters that the modems on each side of the connection have been told to use are so completely incompatible that there is no way meaningful communication can take place on any level, you simply cannot connect to that modem. This is rare and usually points to the lower-level substrates of the connection. The chances of you running into this are very slim indeed.

You Make a Connection That Immediately Goes Away

It is much more likely that you will see severe problems crop up in this manner. If your CD (Carrier Detect, for those of you that went through Sections 2 and 3 too quickly) is set too low, you may drop the connection before the other modem has a chance to respond.

If the two modems are simply talking different languages, they will connect, you will hear all that lovely squealing and whining as they try to find common ground, but it will never get quiet. The connection will time out.

For example, if your modem is looking for DTR (Data Terminal Ready) to be sent by the other modem and it is configured to send a carrier and wait for your modem to send RTS (Ready To Send) before sending DTR, you're hosed.

Basic modem communication that adheres to the standards set forth in RS-232 and the Hayes suite is not usually subject to such whims. These standards specify what is to be sent and in what order, so as long as you bought a Hayes-compliant modem you should not run into this, either.

You Get Gibberish

Now, *this* you may well experience at one time or another. If you're going to become a computer-communications wizard, make the decision ahead of time to have fun with things like this. Look at it as a puzzle to be solved.

If you have good communications software, you should be able to change parameters on-the-fly, without dropping your misbehaving connection. As stated previously, baud rate is unlikely to be the problem, so you only have a couple of things to play with.

Take a close look at the stream you're receiving. Is it really gibberish? Can you detect any patterns at all? If, for example, you see something like this: "LLOOGGIINN IINNCCOORRRREECCTT PPLLEEAASSEE RREETTRRYY," you can probably figure that you configured your modem to echo, when your software usually handles that for you. If they're both echoing, things can look pretty strange.

How about if things are really bizarre, though? True gibberish, with absolutely no discernible pattern to the stream.

If your parity is not set correctly, or if you have too many/few data bits set, this is what you're likely to see. After all, it's not like trying to figure out what someone's written when you're missing the last character of the word, which is comparatively easy. Changing these parameters does more than add/drop a bit from a word. It totally changes the definition of what we mean by a word.

Let's look at what we're talking about here. Compare the results we get by sending "01001001," eight data bits, no parity, with the same stream sent using seven data bits, odd parity. (If we used even parity, we'd get an error and retransmission over and over. Know why?)

Using eight data bits, no parity, we get a word that looks like this: 01001001. This is $0X49_{HEXADECIMAL}$, which translates to an "I" in straight ASCII.

Using seven data bits, odd parity, we get a word that look like this: 0100100. The trailing "1" is assumed to be there to make the word come out odd. This is 0X24$_{HEXADECIMAL}$, which translates to "$" in straight ASCII.

HINT: If you see a lot of characters in your input stream that you almost never see outside of an ASCII table (things like ç, Æ, and ¥), this is probably what ails you. Play with the values, press <Enter> and see what you get back.

HAYES COMPATIBILITY

In many ways modems are like horses and children. In order to have them do what you want, you must first get their attention. In the case of modems it is significantly easier than in either of the analogous cases.

Commanding

To get a modem's attention, you send it a string that it recognizes as "Yo! Listen up." The Hayes-compatible "Yo! Listen up" string is "AT." So, to send a command to a modem and have it notice, you prefix the command with the string AT.

To dial a number, the command is a "D" (this probably stands for "dial"—don't you think?) followed by the type of dialing desired (i.e., T for tone, or P for pulse). So, if you want your modem to dial information for the Denver area and damage the hearing of some poor soul working for US WEST, you would send it the string "ATDT3035551212."

This says, in pidgin-modem, "Yo! Listen up. Call the number (303) 555-1212 using tone dialing."

Of course, once you have the modem's attention you can tell it to do all sorts of things. The following table describes some of the basic Hayes-compatible modem control commands:

Command	Description
A	Answer the phone immediately
En	Command echo
Hn	Hang up
Ln	Speaker volume
Mn	Speaker status (on/off)
Qn	Result codes
Vn	Digit/text result codes
Xn	Extended result codes
Z	Reset
&C	Force DCD
&Dn	DTR modes
&Sn	DSR states

Registers

Many people blanch and feel faint at the mention of the term "register." It would seem to be either a means of checking out of a grocery store or a deep, dark secret based on knowledge long lost to the world of humans. Not so.

A register is a file drawer (well-labeled) that a computer or modem can store things in and later look in to find the data it put there. When you configure your modem, you tell it things like on what ring to answer a call, how long to wait for a carrier before giving up, how long to wait after the carrier is lost before giving up, etc. It has to put that information somewhere. Once it has that information, is has to keep track of how reality is matching up to what it has been told to look for.

For example, you tell your modem to answer the phone on the fourth ring. It has to put the number 4 in a place that it recognizes as the place to look for how many rings to wait before answering. Once it has done this, it must have a place to put the number of rings it has actually heard so that it can do a comparison, decide when your criteria are met, and answer the phone.

Let's say your modem puts the number of rings to wait in a register called S0 and the actual number of rings experienced in one called S1. The phone rings. Your modem increments register S1 from 0 to 1 and compares the value to the value in register S0. Four is more than one, so it doesn't answer the phone. So on with the second and third rings. On the fourth ring it increments S1 to 4, compares it to S0 and gets a match. It answers the phone.

The following table describes some of the basic Hayes-compatible modem register definitions:

Register	Description
S0=n	Auto answer ring count
S1=n	Ring counter
S2=n	Escape code character
S3=n	Carriage return character
S4=n	Line feed character
S5=n	Backspace character
S6=n	Dial wait time value
S7=n	Carrier detect wait time value
S8=n	Dial pause wait time
S9=n	Carrier detect response time
S10=n	Carrier disconnect wait time

Isn't that amazing? Your modem actually DOES use S0 and S1 for just those purposes. You can find out more about this in your modem manual or in your software documentation if you are so inclined.

For most of us, though, this is not the fun part. The fun part begins in the next section, when we delve into the many options available to the intrepid modem wizard.

Section 7

NOW THAT I'M CONNECTED, WHERE CAN I GO?

We've covered all the basics of getting your modem connected and configured, your software installed, your phone hooked up. So now what? Why did you go through all this, buy and actually read this book, spend big bucks on a greased-lightning modem, and learn all sorts of things most people find quite distasteful? To get connected. To surf the Internet, ride the cyberspace wave. To become one with the datasphere.

Then again, maybe you want to make your own plane reservations. It's all out there waiting to be accessed. What you do with it is up to you. To assist you in deciding which direction to take on the information superhighway (one of the few concepts in recent years to become trite before becoming reality) we have put together a summation of what sort of things are out there and how to get to them. In Section 8 we'll look at access providers; what kinds there are and what each kind offers. In Section 9 we'll dance around in the Internet, checking out the incredibly varied options just begging to be tapped into. In Section 10 we get serious again, talking about the Internet addressing scheme, which will without a doubt change as soon as we go to print. Section 11 continues the serious vein with a discussion of protocols. Section 12 is an answer to those who always ask "Where can I find out more?" To quote several famous people appearing at the end of television miniseries, "You can read more about it!" We show you where to find the resources you need to get really obsessive about being on-line.

AN OVERVIEW OF ACCESS OPTIONS

For simplicity's sake, access options can be broken down into three basic categories: DAPs, FAPs, and SAPs.

Direct Access Providers (DAPs)

This is the purist's way to get connected. You hook up your modem, dial your number, and get a UNIX command prompt. No frills, no menus, no "Welcome to VistaSurferWare, the friendly access service!" In many cases, typing "help" won't do a darn thing. This is the service for those who already have a pretty good idea of what's going on and how to get involved.

DAPs often have a very extensive selection of tools you can use to surf the net. If this sort of connectivity interests you, make sure you read on, learn all you can about what tools are out there, which ones interest you, and find out from the companies offering this service which of the tools they offer.

To be fair, not all DAPs offer a huge selection of tools, and not all are this bleak at sign-on. In fact, nearly all of them will put a message from the system administrator on your screen when you sign on, pointing you to new additions, README files, etc. Remember at the beginning of this heading it said, "For simplicity's sake?" You get the general idea.

What you actually have at a DAP is an account on a (probably large) UNIX-based machine that has a high-bandwidth connection to an Internet nexus.

Huh?

Okay. The Internet will be discussed later. Suffice it to say that there are places all over the country where it is possible to tap into the main artery of the Internet. This kind of connection is by far the most efficient, carries the most data, and returns your information-gathering results faster than any other. If you are hungry for data, have a reasonable amount of computer-savvy, and like to learn while zipping about from machine to machine, from Germany to New Zealand to Huntsville to L.A., this is, without the slightest doubt, the way to go.

Friendly Access Providers (FAPs)

Not all FAPs are analogous to VistaSurferWare. In fact, the most popular and successful services are to be found in this category. Services like CompuServe and PRODIGY are the quintessential FAPs. There are many more, and more still are springing up all the time. Signing on to an FAP gets you a welcome screen, a menu, often voice-overs, multi-media glitz, and lots of on-line help. After you get to know your way around, this gets very tedious. (Most serious hackers will bare their teeth at the sound of the word "menu.")

Because of this, most FAPs implement hot keys, or ways to get around the menus and directly to where you need to be.

There are some drawbacks to this approach. FAPs are not cheap. As with most other things, one tends to pay for convenience. Also, these are "information services," not just Internet-access methods. You pay for the overhead of keeping the Cooking With Library Paste SIG happy, running thirty-five simultaneous multi-user dungeons (MUDs), and keeping twenty-seven virtual-reality chat rooms open for those people without even the semblance of a life, too.

The primary thing to consider is: what do you want to do with your access time? If chat rooms, special interest group forums, and e-mail are your cup o' tea, then maybe this is a good choice.

All of these things are accessible directly through the net with a little effort, of course. Well, maybe more than a *little* effort, but definitely accessible. On the flip side, access to the Internet via an FAP can be exceedingly expensive. For someone who spends a great deal of time on the Internet, this access method can be more expensive than buying a private line to an Internet nexus. Watch out, and make sure you know what you're getting for your money.

It is only natural that you would detect a little bias in this section, so here's the disclaimer: FAPs have hundreds of thousands of deliriously happy customers, and there's a reason for it. Not everyone has the time or the energy to put into becoming a net surfer. Even if you think you might, an FAP is a good place to start out.

Specialized Access Providers (SAPs)

Some providers put all their efforts behind one service and make their way in the world by providing that service better and more completely (or simply more cheaply) than any full-featured service could. Thus you can find services that provide you with only the latest stock quotes, or only perform searches of legal databases, or only send and receive electronic mail.

These services are, of course, very handy, but somewhat limiting for the adventurous. You may well want to subscribe to one of these services, but probably not *only* one.

SAPs cater more to the business user, for whom direct, immediate access to every iota of information available (or stock quotes no more than a couple of seconds old) can mean success or failure.

A BREAKDOWN OF SERVICE VALUE CRITERIA

Fees

Everybody charges you to connect you with the world, but no two services figure their fees in exactly the same way. There are startup costs, monthly access charges, minimum connection times, etc. Some mail providers charge only for messages sent. Some services pay you back for having a good modem and advanced software packages by charging you only for data transmission time. Read the fine print, take them up on any free hours offered and see how it goes. If you have one in your area, take advantage of the free-access nets (if you want to check this out, look in Section 8 for a free-access net near you).

E-mail

This is one of the most popular features offered by on-line service providers. In fact, you will be hard-pressed to find a service that does *not* offer e-mail. A worthy e-mail system can provide binary-file attachment, priority delivery, delivery receipts, and mailing lists. Nearly every on-line commercial service provides an e-mail interface to the net, which means that anyone can send to and receive from anyone, no matter what service you or they are using. If the service you're considering doesn't, you can do better. Keep looking.

Informational Databases

Newspapers, magazines, and financial/consumer information services are very attractive resources available on most on-line commercial service providers. Some of these services will cost you over and above your usual connection fees. Make sure you're comparing apples to apples.

News and Financial

News feeds provide both national and international information on a near-real-time basis, including weather forecasts. Some examples of news feeds include the Associated Press and USA Today. Some financial information feeds provide real-time stock quotes, broker services, corporate information, and miscellaneous fund rates. Some of these services will cost you, but when you compare that cost to the advantages of getting your daily paper in electronic format, instantly zooming to the sections that interest you, cutting your recycling pile in half and saving thousands of trees into the bargain, the cost is negligible.

Entertainment

A vast number of people have hobbies and trades that they would like to share with others within the on-line service community. These range from the latest ham-radio news to travel experiences, multi-player on-line games, and, well, the Internet is a big place: you can find almost anything if you look far enough. Most of these resources exist within some sort of discussion area or forum. Some on-line providers actually maintain a library of text of past discussions on various topics, so you can see if you want to tune in for the next debate.

Electronic Chat

Believe it or not, there are people out there who, whether for entertainment or edification or what, routinely sign on and spend their connect time hanging out in virtual rooms talking (typing) to other, like-minded people. There are, in fact, people whose job it is to do so, and act as a sort of host/ess for the room. So, if you're into VRO (Virtual Reality Oprah), it's out there.

Caveats

As previously stated, the Internet is a big place. It has a lot in common with major metropolitan centers in that it has many, many people, doing many, many things, at all hours of the day and night. After all, if you're talking to someone in a chat room you have no idea whether they are down the block or Down Under. Time becomes somewhat subjective at this point.

(If there are six people in a chat room from six different time zones, what time is it in the room? Life just continually gets weirder, doesn't it?)

Some services do mail better than others, or at least there are fewer "gotchas" with some than with others. I have had much more luck sending binary attachments to MCImail account holders than to people using CompuServe. Of course, MCImail just does mail: they *ought* to do it better.

Now that we've determined that there are lots of cool places to go, let's take a look at some different ways to get there.

Section 8

WHAT KINDS OF COMMERCIAL
SERVICES ARE AVAILABLE?

Twenty years ago there were information services, too. Some, like the people who put out the Encyclopedia Britannica, concentrated on giving people a little information on nearly everything (the term "encyclopedic" meaning literally "well-rounded"). Others, mostly professional research companies, concentrated on giving you everything there was on a particular topic.

(In the movie *Desk Set*, Katherine Hepburn plays the manager of just such a service, and Spencer Tracy the efficiency/computer expert who comes in to replace her staff with a room full of spinning tapes and blinking lights. The computer can answer bunches of questions faster that the humans can look them up, but they never talk about how the computer is accessing the information. Someone had to type all that stuff into a database, except of course they couldn't, since when the movie was made the concept of "database" was barely alive, and programming consisted of punching holes in cards. This movie is a fun watch, though.)

Be that as it may, if you wished to form your own information service, you would have some choices to make. Would you pick an area of coverage and provide everything there was to be found? Or would you instead take the approach of providing a smattering of information about everything on the planet? This decision could be called choosing a spot on the information-orientation continuum.

The companies discussed in the following pages have had to make a similar decision. In some cases they chose well and now provide a valuable service to many people. In some cases, they try to go both directions and end up doing neither one well.

In some cases, they don't try. That's the difference between an information service and an access provider. The choices available to you here are many and varied, but mostly point you in the same direction. If you seek information, you can sign up with an information service and get what you want. You can also sign up with an access provider, invest some time and effort (not even money) into the acquisition of some tools (to be discussed in a later section), and wind up in the same place.

DIRECT ACCESS PROVIDERS

These services are really not for the newcomer and definitely not for the faint-at-heart. When you sign on to most of these services you get a UNIX prompt, although some have menus.

Let's say you have a UNIX prompt sitting in front of you. What does this mean? It means you have been given an account on a computer capable of servicing bunches of people at once. You have a sign-on, a home directory, and (maybe very) limited permissions to use the commands available in UNIX to create, delete, upload, download, move, and generally manipulate files in your directory.

That computer will in all probability have facilities for Internet surfing, such as GOPHER, ARCHIE, MOSAIC, FTP, TELNET, IRC, etc. These tools will be discussed in a later section. For now suffice it to say that these tools provide you with all the Internet capability you can get with an information service, but in some cases without the bells and whistles.

This is a way to get access to files. All sorts of neat (and in some instances totally inappropriate for anyone under the age of 75, so be wary of letting children surf unattended) programs, graphic images, databases, games, theses, diatribes, soliloquies, and utilities are out there, sitting around in anonymous FTP sites, waiting for a surfer like you to come and get them. One thing, if you are really into the SIG (Special Interest Group) open forum scene, you'll find more of them, more easily, via one of the FAPs below.

Last note about surfing the net: If you are file-hungry and just got yourself a massive new hard drive you are just aching to fill up with all sorts of stuff, have at it. But before you start, there are two things you should get. First, an anti-virus software package would be a great investment. There is one included with Windows, and until you get a more recent one, definitely use it. Unfortunately, bitter, twisted people are churning out viruses every day, and it would behoove the avid surfer to get the best anti-virus package available and keep getting the updates as they come out. Some of these viruses will utterly destroy the data on your machine, leaving you with a $2,500 doorstop.

This leads us to the second thing you should get, which will save your life if you should miss a virus that really trashes your machine: a tape backup. In fact, we had a drive go south on us in the middle of writing this book and ended up spending almost three times the cost of the tape drive recovering the data that was lost. You can get a good tape backup unit with the software to drive it for under $200. You can configure the software to run a complete backup every Monday morning at 3:00, leave a big fat tape in the drive, and be sure that if you ever get spewed upon by a virus you will lose less than seven days' worth of stuff. You hopefully will never need it, but when you consider the time and money you have invested in your computer, software, and data, $200 and some time setting up the backup scheme is very cheap insurance.

Following, then, is a list of DAPs by state and city. It should in no way be considered exhaustive, and we have not included charges, since the likelihood of them changing as soon as we go to print is too great. If the phone number is a voice line, it is so labeled. If it is a modem line and a first-time guest login is required, we include it.

If your city is not included here or the listing is out-of-date, don't despair. There are at least four companies that provide Internet access on a national level. They will appear at the end of this listing.

ALABAMA

Huntsville **Nuance** Voice: (205) 533-4296

ALASKA

Anchorage **Tundra Services** at the U of A Voice: (907) 465-6453

ARIZONA

Phoenix **Internet Direct** Modem: (602) 274-9600 login id: guest; Voice: (602) 274-0100

Tucson **Data Basics** Modem: (602) 721-5887; Voice: (602) 721-1988

Tucson	**Internet Direct** Modem: (602) 321-9600 login id: guest; Voice: (602) 324-0100

CALIFORNIA

Berkeley	**Holonet** Modem: (510) 704-1058; Voice: (510) 704-0160
Cupertino	**Portal** Modem: (408) 973-8091; Voice: (408) 973-9111
Irvine	**Dial N' CERF** Voice: (800) 876-CERF
LA	**Kaiwan Public Access Internet** Modem: (714) 539-5726; Voice: (714) 638-2139.
	Dial N' CERF Voice: (800) 876-CERF
Oakland	**Dial N' CERF** Voice: (800) 876-CERF
Pasadena	**Dial N' CERF** Voice: (800) 876-CERF
Palo Alto	**Institute for Global Comm.** Modem: (415) 322-0284; login id: new; Voice: (415) 442-0220.
San Diego	**Dial N' CERF** Voice: (619) 534-5087
	CTS Network Services Modem: (619) 637-3660 login id: help; Voice: (619) 637-3637
	Cyberspace Station Modem: (619) 634-1376 login id: guest
San Francisco	**Pathways** Voice: (415) 346-4188
San Jose	**Netcom** Modems: (510) 865-9004 (510) 426-6610 (408) 241-9760 (415) 424-0131 login id: guest; Voice: (408) 554-UNIX.
	A2i Modem: (408) 293-9010 login id: guest
Sausalito	**WELL** Modem: (415) 332-6106 login id: newuser; Voice: (415) 332-4335; Status message: (800) 326-8354

COLORADO

Colorado Springs	**Internet Express** Modem: (719) 570-1700 login id: new; Voice: (719) 592-1240
	Old Colorado City Communications Modem: (719) 632-4111 login id: newuser; Voice: (719) 632-4848
Denver	**Internet Express** Modem: (303) 758-2656 login id: new; Voice: (719) 592-1240

	Denver Free-Net Modem: (303) 270-4865 login id: guest
Other	**Colorado SuperNet** Voice: (303) 273-3471

DELAWARE

Middletown	**Systems Solutions** Modem: (302) 378-1881; Voice: (800) 331-1386

FLORIDA

Talahassee	**Talahassee Free-Net** Modem: (904) 488-5056; Voice: (904) 488-5056.

GEORGIA

Atlanta	**Netcom** Modem: (404) 758-0101

ILLINOIS

Champaign	**Prarienet Free-Net** Modem: (217) 255-9000 login id: visitor; Voice: (217) 244-1962
Chicago	**MCSNet** Modem: (312) 248-0900; Voice: (312) 248-UNIX
Peoria	**Peoria Free-Net** Modem: (309) 674-1100; Voice: (309) 677-2544

MARYLAND

Baltimore	**Express Access** Modems: (410) 766-1855 (301) 220-0462 (714) 377-9784 login id: new; Voice: (800) 969-9090
	Clarknet Modems: (410) 730-9786 (410) 995-0271 (301) 596-1626 (301) 854-0446 login id: guest; Voice: (410) 730-9765

MASSACHUSETTS

Bedford	**The Internet Access Company** Modem: (617) 275-0331; Voice: (617) 275-2221
Brookline	**The World** Modem: (617) 739-9753 login id: new; Voice: (617) 739-0202
Lynn	**North Shore Access** Modem: (617) 593-4557 login id: new; Voice: (617) 593-3110

Worcester   **NovaLink** Modem: (508) 754-4009 login id: info;
Voice: (800) 274-2814

MICHIGAN

Ann Arbor   **MSEN** Voice: (313) 998-4562

Elsewhere   **Michnet** Voice: (313) 764-9430

NEW HAMPSHIRE

Manchester   **MV Communications, Inc.** Voice: (603) 429-2223

NEW JERSEY

New   **Digital Express** Modem: (908) 937-9481 login id:
Brunswick   new; Voice: (800) 969-9090

NEW YORK

New York   **Echo** Modem: (212) 989-8411 login id: newuser;
Voice: (212) 255-3839

Maestro Modem: (212) 240-9700 login id: newuser;
Voice: (212) 240-9600

MindVox Modem: (212) 989-4141 login id: guest;
Voice: (212) 989-2418

Panix Modem: (212) 787-3100 login id: newuser;
Voice: (212) 877-4854

Pipeline Modems: (212) 267-8606 (212) 267-7341
login id: guest; Voice: (212) 267-3636

NORTH CAROLINA

Charlotte   **Vnet Internet Access** Modems: (704) 347-8839
(919) 406-1544 login id: new; Voice: (704) 374-0779

Elsewhere   **Rock Concert Net** Voice: (919) 248-1999

OHIO

Cleveland   **Cleveland Free-Net** Modem: (216) 368-3888
Voice: (216) 368-8737

Wariat Modem: (216) 481-9436 Voice: (216)
481-9428

Cincinnati   **Tri-State Free-Net** Modem: (513) 579-1990

Dayton	**Freelance Systems Programming** Modem: (513) 258-7745; Voice: (513) 254-7246
Lorain	**Lorain County Free-Net** Modems: (216) 277-2359 (216) 366-9753; Voice: (216) 366-4200
Medina	**Medina Free-Net** Modems: (216) 723-6732 (216) 225-6732 (216) 335-6732
Youngstown	**Youngstown Free-Net** Modem: (216) 742-3072

OREGON

Portland	**Agora** Modems: (503) 293-1772 (503) 293-2059 login id: apply **Teleport** Modems: (503) 220-0636 (503) 220-1016 login id: new; Voice: (503) 223-4245

PENNSYLVANIA

Pittsburgh	**Telerama** Modem: (412) 481-5302 Voice: (412) 481-3505

RHODE ISLAND

E.Grnwich	**IDS World Network** Modem: (401) 884-9002
Providence	**Anomaly** Modem: (401) 331-3706 Voice: (401) 273-4669

TEXAS

Austin	**RealTime Comm.** Modem: (512) 459-4391 login id: new; Voice: (512) 451-0046
Dallas	**Texas Metronet** Modems: (214) 705-2901 (817) 261-1127 login id: info or signup; Voice: (214) 705-2900 (817) 543-8756
Houston	**The Black Box** Modem: (713) 480-2686; Voice: (713) 480-2684

VIRGINIA

Norfolk	**Wyvern Technologies** Modem: (804) 627-1828; Voice: (804) 622-4289
Peninsula	**Wyvern Technologies** Modem: (804) 886-0662; Voice: (804) 622-4289

WASHINGTON, DC

The Meta Network Voice: (703) 243-6622

CapAccess Modem: (202) 785-1523 login id: guest password: visitor; Voice: (202) 994-4245

WASHINGTON STATE

Seattle   **Halcyon** Modem: (206) 382-6245 login id: new; Voice: (206) 955-1050

                  Eskimo North Modems: (206) 367-3837 (206) 362-6731; Voice: (206) 367-7457

NATIONAL

Delphi Voice: (800) 695-4005

BIX Voice: (800) 695-4775

PSI Voice: (800) 82PSI82 or (703) 620-6651

NovX Systems Integration Voice: (206) 447-0800

FRIENDLY ACCESS PROVIDERS

CompuServe

CompuServe Information Service (CIS) is the quintessential FAP. It has been around the longest, is by far the largest, and if you're into SIG forums you don't want to be anywhere else. CIS provides a vast pool of resources, including forums, databases, file libraries, and unlimited access to just about everything; news feeds, stock quotes, various reference areas, travel and shopping services, games, and a plethora of interactive forums. To get to all this, CIS provides a navigation software package, CompuServe Information Manager (CIM). CIS also provides several methods of electronic mailing. It handles local mail within the CompuServe environment and has interfaces to the outside world for Internet, fax, telex, and post. CIS also provides gateways to other network services, such as the Internet and ZiffNet. CIS got a jump on everyone over a decade ago, and no one has come close to catching up yet. It is the obvious choice for the data-hungry.

PRODIGY

The PRODIGY interactive on-line service is more family-oriented in nature. The result of a partnership between IBM and Sears, Roebuck and Co., it remains the ultimate home user service, with services ranging from sports to cooking. The user interface has a very intuitive look: well organized and very graphic intensive. Because of the graphic-intensive interface, it tends to be a little slow, depending on the baud rate supported by the local access point and your modem's capabilities.

PRODIGY provides an exceptional research library for families that includes major encyclopedias, consumer reports, and political information. PRODIGY also contains a type of electronic newspaper. Bulletin boards and electronic mail were designed for exchanging information and ideas between users.

In a nutshell, PRODIGY is a great service for people with a smaller appetite for information, especially those with children.

America Online

America Online (AOL) is a relative newcomer to the information service field, and the offering of information retrieval mechanisms is by no means its forte. AOL offers limited business and financial services, news feeds, magazines, newspapers, and research services. The interfaces to the electronic mail system, file transfer libraries, and forums are very intuitive and easy to use. The primary service that AOL offers that you won't find just anywhere is what they call "the People Connection." These are virtual chat rooms. (I just signed on to AOL and went into the "lobby" of the chat department. It is 12 noon on a Saturday. There were 23 people in the lobby. I did not go into any of the chat rooms, of which there were about 25.) AOL allows the holder of the master account to set up limits on what rooms can be entered, so you can control what sorts of conversations your children participate in when you're not around.

SPECIALIZED ACCESS PROVIDERS

MCImail

MCImail is a service that provides electronic mail. The service interfaces with a multitude of other electronic mail systems, such as

X.500 and the Internet. MCImail also provides a fax, telex, and postal (a.k.a. snail mail) service for your electronic communications. Some of the unique features of the electronic mail system include group lists, return receipt, and priority transmission. MCImail provides an interface to Dow Jones News/Retrieval for current stock and financial information, as well as a Wall Street Journal service.

MCImail is the country's largest electronic mail service provider.

In addition to the above services, we sent requests, both electronic and physical, to the following entities:

- ATT Personal Link
- Ziff-Davis Interchange
- Apple On-line Services

None of them ever got back to us, so there isn't a great deal we can tell you about them, although perhaps their lack of responsiveness speaks for itself.

Microsoft is expanding its hold on the western world by including Internet capability with Windows 95. We have not yet seen this, so we cannot comment on its efficacy.

One of the things we mentioned again and again in this section was Internet access. Should that be a deciding factor for your selection of a service? After all, when we talk about a DAP, FAP, or SAP, the "Access" part refers to the Internet. Let's take a look at why this might be important to you.

Section 9

I KEEP HEARING ABOUT THE INTERNET. WHAT'S THE BIG DEAL?

The Internet is the largest collection of networks in the world. It includes networks pretty much everywhere in the world. The world, as we know, is a very large place. Electrons travel pretty darn quickly, but even if we're talking 30,000,000 meters/sec, working on a machine halfway around the world is going to take a certain amount of patience. Of course, even that is changing. Now that much of the physical transport medium of the Internet is being replaced with fiberoptic cable, transport speeds are getting very close to the cruising speed of a photon, and the world isn't big enough to notice geographic displacement.

What all this means is an English-speaking Internet surfer in Kyoto can be signed on to a chat room, along with a user from Sydney, one from Singapore, one from Berlin, one from Edinburgh, and a couple from various parts of the USA, and no one would be able to tell they weren't right next-door, apart from the tell-tale differences in grammar and idiom.

One hundred years ago, if you needed access to the contents of a file that existed only in Mozambique, you would have waited the better part of a year to get the word to whomever (or, more probably, get there yourself) and get the file back to you. For the privilege of making this journey, you would pay somewhere upwards of a year's wages for a master carpenter.

Fifty years ago, the scenario would have been pretty similar, substituting propeller-driven airplanes for wooden ships, and "month" for "year."

Twenty-five years ago jets would have reduced that trip to a couple of days, but the cost would still be exorbitant. (You could have relied on the two countries' postal services in any of these cases, but let's assume you were serious about getting it as soon as possible.)

Now, you sign on to your local access provider, FTP to the machine holding the file in Mozambique, go to the appropriate directory, and type in the command "get *<filename>*." Depending on the size of the file and the speed of your connection, you have your file in a matter of seconds or minutes, totally reliably, without involving anyone else, without leaving your chair, for pennies.

What if you just need to see if the word "rosebud" appears in the second paragraph? Instead of FTPing to the Mozambique machine, you TELNET to it, sign on, type in "more *<filename>*," and read the second paragraph. Now we're talking pennies, scant seconds, sign off, and you're on your way.

Let's not lose sight of some facts: first, it does cost something to do this; not much in comparison with doing nearly anything else, but there is a cost. Second, the real advantage to all this is the removal of geographic boundaries to data gathering. It is just as easy to get the file from Outer Mongolia as it is to get it from the local university, assuming you have a valid login id and password.

Third and most important, what we've been talking about so far is so rudimentary it's pathetic. The power of the Internet is not just the removal of geographic boundaries; that's just the key that unlocks the door (or, more appropriately, opens the floodgates in preparation for the tsunami).

We'll spend the rest of the section discussing the software that makes use of this fabulously fertile intellectual medium, and makes it not just possible, but EASY to gather data concerning nearly anything, from nearly anywhere, without even having to figure out where anywhere is!

ELECTRONIC MAIL

One of the most popular things that being connected to the Internet provides is the ability to send messages to others connected to the net. For all intents and purposes, e-mail is just like postal mail, except that it tends to arrive at your destination within a matter of seconds, can be sent to as many people as you wish simply by adding them to the header of the message, and can be sent to fax machines for those who haven't yet gotten connected. E-mail can also be used to communicate with a special server called a mail server. This is a computer that processes your requests and then mails you back a response (most of the time—this is one of the ways we attempted to get information from the services mentioned in the previous section).

The format of an electronic mail message is similar to that of a postal mail letter. With postal mail, you need a name and a physical address to which the letter should be delivered. With e-mail you need a user id and a logical address. With e-mail, you have the option of CCing other people, but postal mail requires an individual letter per recipient.

(Wait a minute here. I don't know how many of you out there have used e-mail, but the term CC has always bugged me. For crying out loud, it stands for "carbon copy!" We have many holdovers from the days of typewriters, which includes our keyboards and our tendency to put white-out on our monitor screens, but a reference to carbon paper is going too far.)

E-mail messages have the return address attached to the message, along with some details about how it got to its destination. If you're ever bored and looking for something to do, look at some old messages and check out the places they passed through on their merry way to your desktop. You'll be surprised.

ELECTRONIC JOURNALS AND NEWSLETTERS

Electronic journals and newsletters are (of course) similar to their printed cousins, except that they (of course) are stored and distributed as computer data or text. As with printed magazines, you subscribe to have a certain number of issues "mailed" to you.

Unlike printed magazines, you can electronically search for interesting topics, easily delete advertisements, add editorial comments and emphasis, print out those pieces that you want in hard-copy, and not get buried in old dead trees.

ON-LINE LIBRARY CATALOGS

Many libraries around the world are now accessible to anyone connected to the Internet, at any time, day or night. Essentially, the libraries have put their card catalogs into a computer database, which in turn provides an electronic card catalog interface. Users may search for materials by subject, title, or author. Some even offer detailed bibliographic information about each book.

Some services can arrange to transfer a book to a branch close to you, or if you're really serious about convenience, you can use these services to find the book you want, then go and see if the folks at Project Gutenberg have put it on-line yet.

WIDE AREA INFORMATION SERVER (WAIS)

The Wide Area Information Server (WAIS) is a collection of information servers that provide users easy, transparent access to information. In a nutshell, WAIS is based on two ideas: "content navigation" and "dynamic folders."

Content navigation means that you specify a search to WAIS along the lines of "Show me all files concerning the sport of ferret legging." WAIS then goes out and searches all files (you can narrow the search to particular servers if you wish) in its domain, and that is a seriously large number of files, and reports back to you with a list of files ordered by the number of times the term "ferret legging" appears in each. (If you think I'm kidding, try it sometime. Then read the articles you find. You'll be a better, happier person for it.)

A collection of files is generally referred to as a folder, especially in the Mac world and often in e-mail facilities. The previous search yielded nothing more than a collection of files, so we can think of it as a folder. A dynamic folder, then, is one in which you can specify search criteria as above, but add, "re-check for updates and additions once a week." You could also say, "re-check every time a file is saved on server Oouagadugu." Your folder then becomes an agent (that's what this sort of thing is called in CompuServe) that acts, completely without your intervention, to keep you up-to-date on the latest happenings in the world of ferret legging.

WAIS is not a service. It is not owned by any one company. It is supported by many different companies and universities, and grows larger daily.

DIRECTORY SERVICES

The Internet provides a facility to obtain information about people and companies. This is equivalent to using the white pages to locate a user or a host and yellow pages to locate Internet services. These directory services include:

- X.500 directory services
- MCImail
- Whois utility
- Finger utility
- Knowbot Information Server (KIS)

The Knowbot Information Server is located at info.cnri.reston.va.us, and is open for anyone's use. Simply TELNET to the address (no password is needed) and put your name in the "guest book." You may then type in a name, and off it will scurry, querying whois servers at ds.internic.net, rs.internic.net, mcimail.com, nic.ddn.mil, whois.ripe.net, and whois.lac.net.

You'll be amazed at what you will find, with so little effort.

WORLD WIDE WEB (WWW)

WWW started with a company called CERN, which translates to "European Laboratory for Particle Physics." The Europeans were pretty far ahead of the Americans when it came to networking their information servers together in a standard way. The WWW project works as a WAIS. There are browsers available for harvesting information regardless of your machine type or configuration. If you can FTP, (and anyone on the Internet can FTP) you can download a browser and start taking advantage of WWW.

What the heck am I talking about? I know, it all seems like black magic sometimes, but really, there is nothing supernatural going on. There are anonymous FTP sites out there...

(Okay, an anonymous FTP site is a computer that sits around answering the phone all day, has a great deal of disk space, lots of files, and lets anyone in that wants in. To sign on to an anonymous FTP site, type something like "ftp anon.ftp.site.com" (no, there is no such site, we'll list a bunch of them later on) and wait for a connection. You will be prompted for a login name. Type "anonymous" and wait for the password prompt. At that prompt, type your Internet address. You're in.)

...that hold programs you can download to your machine. Some of these sites hold programs called browsers. Once downloaded, you can run these browsers and they will go out and find information servers to query for the information you seek. Some of those servers will point the way to other servers, etc., etc. The generic name for these programs is browsers, because they collect information and allow you to browse through it. What they are really is data harvesters, and there are a few of them out there, specialized for different types of servers on the net. Let's look at a few.

DATA HARVESTERS

Archie

Archie is a collection of resource discovery tools that form the basis of an electronic directory service for the Internet. When it started, Archie tracked the contents of anonymous FTP sites. Archie now includes a variety of other on-line directories and resource listings and is quickly becoming pervasive.

If you have a direct connection to the Internet, you can access an Archie server interactively. If not, (and this is *really* cool) you can send an Archie server a request for information via e-mail and it will perform your query, package your response, and mail it back to you.

If you have Internet access, you can find an interactive Archie server on the host "archie.mcgill.ca" [132.206.2.3]. TELNET to this host and login as user "archie" (there is no password needed). You'll see a banner message giving latest developments and information on the Archie project and then you'll get a command prompt. Type "help" for information on the service.

If all you have is e-mail, send a message to "archie@archie.mcgill.ca" with the single word "help" in the subject line. You should soon receive an e-mail message explaining how to use the e-mail Archie server and its variants.

The Archie server archie.mcgill.ca is an anonymous FTP site, so you can also FTP there and download Archie client software, found in the subdirectory archie/clients. There are several such clients and more are being tested all the time. Details are posted in the Archie banner message displayed on login.

Documentation for Archie is available for anonymous FTP from the same host under the directory "archie/doc."

Gopher

Gopher was developed in April 1991 by the University of Minnesota Microcomputer, Workstation, Networks Center to help their students find answers to their computer questions. It has since grown into the largest worldwide information system in use today.

When I first started up Gopher on my machine at work, I had no idea what to expect. I told it to show me all the Gopher servers in the world. I waited for close to ten minutes while literally every Gopher server in the world raised its hand and said, "Here I am!" to my machine.

Once this was done (and you only need to do it once in a while, to pick up recent additions) I was a click away from scanning or downloading information from pretty much anywhere in the world.

A Gopher server is a machine someone has set up to respond to the Gopher protocol, making all of its data available to anyone running a Gopher client. Gopher servers work together, providing both a distributed data delivery system for local data and links which facilitate access to other information servers all around the world. Unlike WAIS, which utilizes content navigation and dynamic folders, Gopher simply shows you a tree structure representing the geographic areas, the servers in those areas, the directories on those servers, and the files in those directories. You must search for what you need. If you ever find yourself with several hours to kill, just get on Gopher and start looking at stuff. The time will pass without your being aware of it.

To run Gopher, you will of course need a Gopher client. These are available for nearly any computer out there, and (naturally) are free for the asking. Just FTP to the anonymous FTP site "boombox.micro.umn.edu" (134.84.132.2) and look in the directory "/pub/gopher."

In that directory you will find the following subdirectories containing Gopher clients:

- /pub/gopher/Unix/gopher1.03.tar.Z (Curses & Emacs)
- /pub/gopher/Unix/xgopher1.1a.tar.Z (X)
- /pub/gopher/Mac_client/ (Macintosh Hypercard)
- /pub/gopher/Macintosh-TurboGopher (Macintosh Application)
- /pub/gopher/PC_client/ (DOS w/Clarkson Driver)
- /pub/gopher/NeXT/ (NeXTstep)
- /pub/gopher/Rice_CMS/ (VM/CMS)
- /pub/gopher/Vienna_CMS/ (VM/CMS)
- /pub/gopher/VMS/ (VMS)
- /pub/gopher/os2/ (OS/2 2.0)
- /pub/gopher/mvs/ (MVS/XA)

If you have problems or questions, the people behind the lion's share of Gopher software can be reached via:

E-mail	gopher@boombox.micro.umn.edu
Postal mail	Internet Gopher Developers
	100 Union St. SE #190
	Minneapolis, MN 55455
FAX	(612) 625-6817

Mosaic

Mosaic is one of the most impressive information-gathering tools ever devised. We previously discussed WWW, or World Wide Web. This was a network of information servers that operate on a hypertext algorithm, which simply means that words in a file will be linked to other files containing more information about those topics. Click on the word, go to the other file. It's very cool, but the base interface is rather clunky.

Enter Mosaic. This is a graphical tool that connects to WWW servers (and nearly everything else, it seems) and presents you with more information based on a mouse click or two than you would believe.

The UNIX version is called Mosaic, but there is also a Windows version floating around on Internet called "Netscape." (Note to net surfers connected via PCs with Ethernet connections to UNIX machines providing gateway service to the Internet: If you're running PC-NFS 5.0 or earlier on your Windows box, you're out of luck. Netscape will overwhelm it. You'll have to download Mosaic to your UNIX box, set your display back, and run it that way, or upgrade your PC-NFS.)

Veronica

Do you want Mosaic for your very own? Are you angry with us for not telling you where you can get it? Time to declare your independence and go find it yourself. We will, however, tell you how.

We have discussed Gophers. The data residing on Gopher servers or accessible by them is called Gopherspace.

We have discussed Archie. Archie provides an easy way to navigate around FTP sites, which previously had to be searched through a directory at a time.

Veronica (can you guess why it's called Veronica?) does for Gopherspace what Archie does for FTP sites.

Bring up a Veronica (normally included in your Gopher distribution) and give it the keyword "mosaic."

Have fun.

We have talked about FTP sites and servers galore, either referring to them either by domain name (boombox.micro.umn.edu) or by IP address (134.84.132.2). In the next section we'll look at IP addressing: what it means and how to read it.

In Section 11 we'll look at protocols, the means whereby we move information back and forth across the net. Finally, in Section 12 we'll give you a bunch of places to look for more information.

Let's get to it.

Section 10
WHAT DOES 111.222.111.222 MEAN?

Wait! Don't skip to Section 11! This really isn't that bad, and once you know it, it becomes almost friendly. Really.

Humans don't like hexadecimal. In fact, humans really feel uncomfortable around anything but decimal, and binary makes them ill. Octal is no better, and if you start talking about some of the more arcane bases (36?), people will throw you out of their homes.

Unfortunately, decimal just doesn't work very well where computers and addressing are concerned, so one must grit one's teeth and try to be accepting of other thought patterns. Ready?

WHERE DID ALL THIS COME FROM, AND WHY?

In the beginning, there was ARPANET. This was a rudimentary network connecting a couple of dozen computers around the country, mostly belonging to Department of Defense contractors. ARPA stood for Advanced Research Projects Agency, which before long became DARPA (sticking "Defense" on the front, after the principal funding body), which pretty much paid for the building of the tools and protocols we're discussing here.

These guys needed reliable transmission in and especially between networks. The networks with which they were concerned bore no resemblance to each other (and why would they, when there were no standards to go by?), so starting from scratch they came up with a scheme which (as with the postal addressing scheme) identifies the source and destination of an object, which in this case is called a "datagram."

They called this the "Internet Suite of Protocols."

If you want to send a packet of information from a machine on one network to a machine on another totally different network, you need to have some warm fuzzy mechanisms built in, i.e., some information needs to travel with the data to make you believe that it has a reasonable chance of getting where you send it. In some of these cases you are used to doing this from sending letters via the postal service. In some cases, not.

- Where the packet is going (destination address)
- Where it is coming from (return address)
- How much data is there in the packet (no postal analogy)
- Is this packet associated with other packets? (no postal analogy)
- If so, in what way and in what order? (no postal analogy)
- Error-detection mechanism (certified mail—return receipt requested)

This is all called overhead, and overhead costs money. Therefore, all this information must be included as efficiently as possible, say, in 24 bytes.

That's 192 bits. That's not a lot of room.

Well, they took a third of the space they had and gave that to source and destination addresses. That means we have 32 bits for specifying an address. To make it easier to understand, they broke that up into four octets, like so:

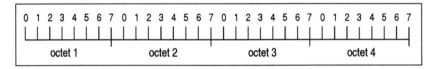

An octet (of course) has 8 bits. If it only had 7 it would be septet, after all. Each of those bits can hold either a 0 or a 1 (binary) like so:

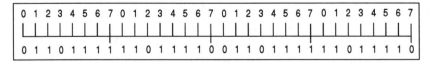

It takes four binary bits to describe a hexadecimal number, i.e., 0000 is still zero when converted to hex, and 1111 = F, or the equivalent of decimal 15. Therefore, we have two hex numbers in each octet.

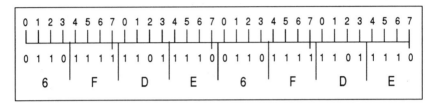

Joining the numbers in each octet, we have a quick and easy conversion to decimal, like so:

$$6F = (6 \times 16) + 15 = (96) + 15 = 111$$

$$DE = (13 \times 16) + 14 = (208) + 14 = 222$$

Separating the value of each octet with a dot (sometimes referred to as *dot notation*, sometime as *dotted quad notation*) we get our 111.222.111.222.

So what does 111.222.111.222 mean? Hang on, we're getting there.

Thirty-two bits, or four octets of eight bits each, gives us four numbers between 00000000 and 11111111BINARY, between 00 and FFHEXADECIMAL, or between 0 and 255. See? Decimal! When are you going to learn to trust me?

Most people find 111.222.111.222 easier to remember than 6FDE6FDE, so dotted quad notation was born. This notation also makes it more intuitive when considering the different classes of IP addresses. There are five, of which no one really needs to know more than three:

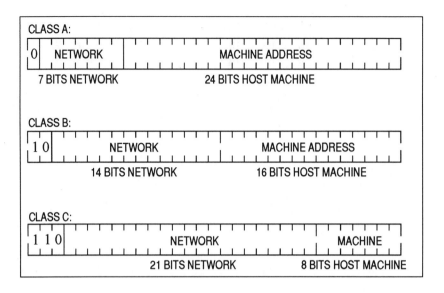

Let's take them in order: Class A licenses are for extremely large corporate entities that have bazillions of machines. The first bit is 0, so we have only 7 bits to specify the network. Therefore, effectively there are only 128 Class A licenses. (Or would be if 127.???.???.??? were not reserved for internal loopback.) Class A licenses are numbered 000.aaa.bbb.ccc through 126.xxx.yyy.zzz. (Except of course all zeros is taken to always refer to the machine to which you're logged on.) Each Class A license contains approximately 16,775,000 machine addresses. (There are 3 octets available to specify a machine address. Each octet contains 8 bits. Each bit can have 2 values: 0 or 1. The value of 2^8 is 256. The value of 256^3 is 16,777,216. Not all addresses are available for reasons similar to the internal loopback caveat above. Rounding off similarly to Intel's first Pentium™ chips, we get 16,775,000.)

Class B licenses are for big companies, with a large number of machines. Because the first bit is 1 and the second is 0, the first octet of a class B address will always be between 128 and 191. This gives us 64 addresses left in the first octet. However, with a Class B license we also have the second octet to use to specify the network, so there are 16,384 Class B licenses (64x256). Each Class B address contains approximately 65,000 machine addresses (65,536 less some reserved numbers).

Class C licenses are for small companies with few machines. Companies often start out with Class C licenses, apply for more of them as they grow, and when they reach a critical point of growth apply for a Class B. Because the first two bits are 1 and the third is 0, Class C licenses start with a number between 192 and 223. Here we also have the second and third octets to specify the network, so there are 2,097,152 Class C licenses, each containing approximately 250 machine addresses.

The problem with this scheme is that the people that came up with it did not anticipate (how could they?) the growth of the personal PC market. Not that we have more machines out there than we have addresses (the theoretical limit of addresses is 256^4, or 4,294,967,296), but the schema is set up so that there is no way to give someone a license for less than 250 machines. There are a large number of companies in the country that got a Class C license to cover their eight machines.

Companies with a couple thousand machines have a nightmare trying to keep track of the 15 or so Class C licenses they got to cover all their addresses, and it's a pain for a growing company to be applying for another Class C every few months, so they apply for a Class B and tie up 65,000 addresses, using less than 10%.

Needless to say, with the advent of worldwide computing and the growth of the Internet, as well as the sheer number of machines out there needing addresses, we will soon see a new IP addressing scheme. (There has already been talk of simply adding two more octets, but that would not solve the basic flaw in the system.) When that happens, look for a second edition of this book soon after.

WHY YOU MOSTLY DON'T HAVE TO WORRY ABOUT THIS

Once upon a time, in a reality far, far away, there was a utility called DNS (Domain Name Service). Its purpose in life was to take care of the numbers so that the poor people didn't have to. It created *domains* (which pretty much means what you think it does), the names of which people could remember, and mapped IP addresses (actually it mapped licenses and pieces of licenses called subnets, but that's splitting hairs) to those domain names.

For example, In The Beginning, there was mit.edu. The convention is simple: domain names are generally all lowercase, with simple descriptors separated by periods. The last descriptor describes the type of organization that is sponsoring the machine. If a name ends with "edu" it is an educational institution. A "com" denotes a commercial enterprise. An "org" tells you the government is behind this one.

So, of course, when the digit-heads at MIT wanted a domain, they called it mit.edu. Naturally, it didn't take long for that domain to get very large and unwieldy, so different departments adopted their own domains, put in their own servers, and created things like cs.mit.edu.

DNS is still being used, but NIS and NIS+ are doing their level-best to supplant it. What the server utility is called and how it does its thing is thankfully not your concern. The important part is that it is done.

Why is this important? This is how e-mail addresses are constructed, too. Fred Garvin has his own domain, that being the address of the house in which he lives, and we address mail to him by giving his name followed by his domain.

E-mail is no different. Fred's e-mail address at the computer science department of MIT would be something like "fred.garvin@cs.mit.edu."

If Fred had an e-mail account through the on-line service DELPHI, his address would be "fred.garvin@delphi.com." If Fred left his current profession to pursue a career with the Federal Bureau of Investigation, his address would be something like "fred.garvin@fbi.org" which would greatly please many people.

This naming convention only holds true in the United States. Geographic boundaries no longer mean anything, so get used to seeing other types of descriptors on the end of Internet addresses. The convention in Europe is to have the last descriptor denote the country in which the machine resides, so you'll see things like ftp_site.uk, ftp_site.fr, and ftp_site.de all over. (P.S.: The "de" means *Deutchland*, or Germany, not Denmark.)

The Europeans do put meaningful descriptors in their domain names, it's just harder for us to read them. Look for "uni" in the middle instead of "edu" at the end, and so on.

Domain names are, to whatever extent possible, descriptive of their nature. Many (though certainly not all) anonymous FTP sites begin with the descriptor "ftp." Many web server names begin with "www."

Now that we know how everybody is addressed, you're probably burning to find out what sorts of things can we do with those addresses and how all of that works. It would be cruel to delay your gratification, so let's look.

Section 11

WHAT'S A PROTOCOL?

A protocol is an agreement. This agreement concerns how business is to be done. My 1978 edition of the Random House Dictionary thinks this is all about international diplomacy, but that's what 16 years will do to you.

Whether we're talking about peace talks in Rangoon, merger negotiations in Boston, or two computers discussing ways of ridding the planet of a certain two-legged infestation, communication depends on the protocols being correct. If the two sides are operating under different assumptions, no understanding is likely to take place.

The protocol for most of the western world says it is mete and proper when one is a guest at another's table to stifle a belch and excuse oneself when done. In other cultures these very same actions would be interpreted as deliberately insulting the quality of the cuisine. People, like machines, are different.

We have described the basics of the Internet Protocol's addressing scheme. We know it consists of 32 bits, broken into four octets of eight bits each. When we write them out on paper, they make some sense, since we are operating under a protocol of our own: read from left to right. Computers don't all read left to right (it would be more proper to write "most-significant bit (MSB) to least-significant bit (LSB)," or big end to little end, but I'm tired of quibbling), so this sort of thing has to be specified in the protocol. In the IP suite, everybody must "read left to right."

INTERNET PROTOCOLS

TCP/IP

You see this a lot in computer circles, and you can measure the RGV (Relative Geek Value) of the person you're talking to by the facility with which it rolls off his/her tongue.

It's not a protocol. It's two protocols that work together. IP, or Internet Protocol, is a connectionless-mode network service, which means that it handles getting the packets to their destination, and addressing is built in. Whether or not the packet got unutterably flummoxed on the way there, IP couldn't care less.

TCP, on the other hand, is a connection-oriented transport protocol that ensures the packet that arrives at the destination is the same as the packet that left the source. Being a connection-oriented protocol, TCP is in essence a state machine. It begins in a closed state, and as events occur it performs an action which causes it to transition to a new state.

So, if you're sending a command to a remote machine via TCP/IP, the first thing you do is establish a connection. Once the connection is established, you have two virtual pipelines for data, one going in each direction.

After a certain number of packets have gone back and forth, you will want to make sure everything is still hunky-dory. The number of packets you want to transmit before doing this is configurable within limits. If you're not a system administrator, don't worry about it.

TCP checks that everything is still copacetic by keeping tabs on the checksum field and checking with the source machine that the checksums are the same. If there is a problem detected, it retransmits the packet.

The cool thing is, this is all transparent to you, the user. The only thing you really have to know is that TCP guarantees the receipt of your packets in their original form. I know you'll sleep easier now.

FTP

We're going into this one quite a bit more deeply, because this may well be the facility you use more than any other when you start surfing the Internet. Thousands of systems on the Internet have public domain file libraries full of free or very cheap programs for nearly any pursuit, for virtually any machine.

But (wo)man does not live by programs alone! Looking for a summary of the latest bill before Congress? It's on the Internet. Need a copy of the Magna Carta? Original or translation? It's on the Internet. Song lyrics from the 60s, 70s, and 80s? No problem. Script summaries of all the *Star Trek* episodes? You bet.

You'll also find files detailing everything anyone could ever want to know about the Internet itself.

FTP can take you there.

Well, sort of. FTP can get you those files. It's up to you to find them. This is precisely the limitation that gave rise to the data harvesters discussed in Section 8. Which of those harvesters handles FTP sites? If you don't know, you haven't been reading carefully.

Let's assume you find the appropriate harvester (Archie—Okay? That's the last time I help you.) and find a summary of David Gerrold's script for the *Star Trek* episode "The Trouble with Tribbles." It's in an anonymous FTP site called ftp.wasted.life.trekkie.heaven.com.

You type in (assuming your system has FTP, which if you are on the Internet is a good bet):

```
ftp ftp.wasted.life.trekkie.heaven.com <Enter>
```

It may take a few seconds (who knows WHERE this place is), but if the connection works you'll see a message telling you to where you're connected. You would also probably get a prompt like the following:

```
Name (ftp.wasted.life.trekkie.heaven:rap):
```

(If it can't establish the connection it'll time out after a minute or so. If you get impatient, or if it takes longer, you can hit <Ctrl+C> to get out.)

Unless you had an account on this machine, and if you're reading this book that seems unlikely, you would type in:

```
anonymous<Enter>
```

Well, of course that's what you'd type. It's an anonymous FTP site, isn't it? That does not actually mean you can remain safely anonymous, though. It is considered good manners to leave a record of who you are when you sign on. Thus, when you are prompted for a password you type in your Internet address. Many anonymous FTP sites will scan your password and if they don't see the telltale signs of an Internet address (characters like "@", ".", etc.) they won't let you in.

Let's assume you have nothing to hide, you type in your Internet address and get into the site. You'll get another message. Depending on the site it could be pitifully dry or as embarrassing as the day is long in summer. You'll be sitting in a guest directory. You have access to a limited set of UNIX commands. Some of those you will find useful are:

- ls—lists contents of directory
- ls -l—lists contents of directory, but tells you everything, including size, which can be important if you want to download something over a 2400 baud line
- pwd—prints the current directory
- cd *<directory-name>*—changes the current directory— remember, UNIX uses "/", not "\" in directory names, but ".." still moves you up one directory level

You will also have access to FTP commands, which is after all how you get anything done. Once you have maneuvered yourself into the correct directory and located your file, you must check the filename you're after to see what kind of file it is. (Many files in sites like this are "zip"ed, or compressed using the utility "pkzip." Naturally, you'll need "pkunzip" to do anything with the file once you've downloaded it. My guess is you'll want to download pkunzip.exe first thing. It's available all over the place and is shareware—if you like it and use it often, as you no doubt will, send the author the fee specified and get stuff like a manual for it, etc. It's well worth the money.)

If the file you seek is in fact a zipfile (ends in ".zip"), the first command you will need to issue is:

```
binary<Enter>
```

to switch to binary transfer mode. There are only two modes, binary and ASCII. If you transfer an executable or compressed file in ASCII mode, it will take three times as long and you'll end up with garbage. You can safely transfer an ASCII file in binary mode, however.

To download a file, you will use FTP commands like the following:

- get <*filename*>—downloads the file specified to your machine
- mget <*filenamelist* -or- *wildcard*>—downloads every file specified or every file matching the wild card, asking if you're sure for each one, which can get to be a drag if you're downloading 40 files
- prompt—how to deal with the mget problem above: turns off the prompt for each file on an mget or mput—you get them all or put them all, no chance to back out in the middle

Uploading a file is similar, substituting "put" for "get" in all cases, but there may be permissions problems, and it is best to leave mail for the system administrator asking if it's okay before you start dumping files onto a strange machine.

Speaking of mail and system administrators, you should be sure to read the README.*WHATEVER* file up at the top of the directory. Most archive sites have at least one "read me" document (often one per major directory), which contains some basic information about the site, its resources and how to use them. It's worth the time.

You will also often find a file called "ls-lR" in one of the uppermost levels of the directory structure. If you're serious about the time you spend on-line, grab that file. The command "ls -lR" gives you a complete listing of everything from the directory in which you sit on down, *R*ecursively, also listing everything in every directory below you. That file contains the listing obtained by issuing that command. It's often very large, but always extremely handy.

OTHER PROTOCOLS

FTP is by far the most popular and most widely used file transfer protocol, but there are others, and if you do any BBS surfing in addition to playing around on the Internet, you'll run into one or all of these. If you haven't read about file transfer protocols in Section 4, here is the information again.

Kermit

Yes, this was named after the famous frog. It started out in the academic world, developed by Frank DaCruz and Bill Catchings at

Columbia University. It is public domain software and is still extremely popular. The complete Kermit manual is available by writing to: Kermit Distribution, Columbia University Center for Computing Activities, 612 West 115th Street, NY, NY 10025.

Xmodem

This file transfer protocol was developed in the mid-1970s by Ward Christensen and placed in the public domain. It was intended for transferring files over 300 and 1200 bps modems connecting CP/M machines. If you were surprised to hear that Paul McCartney was in a band before Wings, you probably have never heard of CP/M. It was one of the very few competitors DOS had before Microsoft conquered the earth. In spite of this, Xmodem's public domain status and general ease of use have kept it popular for a very long time.

Ymodem

There are several flavors of Ymodem. The basic version was written as an extension to Xmodem to get around some of the former's shortcomings. It was designed by Chuck Forsberg to increase the block size from 128 to 1024 bytes and enable the sending of information about the file along with the file itself. One of the variants, YmodemG, sends the whole file before performing any error-checking. If an error is found, the entire file needs to be resent. This works very well in the world of modems with hardware-based error detection.

Zmodem

This is the leading protocol for high-speed file transfers over dial-up lines. It has 32-bit CRC, server functions, batch mode, and the ability to pick up where it left off if it gets unplugged in the middle of a transfer. Zmodem was funded by Telebit, designed by our old friend Chuck Forsberg, and placed in the public domain.

CompuServe B

As the name suggests, this protocol is for exchanging files with the access provider CompuServe.

Finger

Finger is sort of like TELNET and FTP, but it works with only one file, called ".plan." This is a file you can create in your home directory, putting in your phone number, home address, preferred house pets, number of Mexican tarantulas on your ceiling, or pretty much anything at all.

Why, you ask?

Good question. Probably the best answer is that the people with the smarts and the perseverance to discover your Internet address and the knowledge to finger you (pardon the way that sounds) to find these things out may well be people you would enjoy knowing better.

To finger somebody, you just type:

```
finger <e-mail address>
```

You'll get back some info, like the last time the person was on-line, whether they've gotten any new mail since then, and what strange messages they placed there for intrepid hackers like yourself to find.

You have the basic idea. You know about the tools. Your modem is warmed up and ready to go. All you need is some idea of where to start your odyssey. Luckily, that is the subject of Section 12.

Section 12

HOW DO I FIND OUT MORE?

The Internet, like any major advancement in technology, is only as good as the tools available to allow one to take advantage of it. You've been hearing all about the amazing things you can find with a little perseverance. Here is where we shorten the learning curve a little.

In this section we'll list as much of what you can find as we can reasonably do in a few pages. The beauty of the Internet is that most of the sites you encounter there will point you to more sites.

Once you have amassed a respectable collection of tools, you will no longer care about sites *per se*, you will simply tell your tools what you want and let them find it for you. Until then, here are some places to go prospecting. We have wherever possible included the Internet address (as opposed to the IP address), the general subject matter, and availability. Toward the end, we also point you to the next level, telling you where to find tools that ride the big waves.

A ROADMAP TO BASIC SERVICES

Bulletin Boards

We've ordered these by area code for your convenience in finding one relatively close to you. These are some of the top services in the country as of press time.

Synergy On-line	(201) 331-1797
Starship Enterprise	(201) 283-1806
Starship 2	(201) 935-1485
Laser Connection	(201) 472-7785
Bytes'n Bits	(201) 437-4355
GearBox	(201) 692-1110

Mission Fun House	(203) 374-0101
Download America	(203) 676-1708
Northern Lights	(207) 761-4782
Public Access	(209) 277-3008
The Castle	(213) 953-0040
Chrysalis	(214) 690-9295
HyperLinc East	(215) 356-1630
RunWay	(215) 623-6203
Glass Menagerie	(215) 376-1819
PC-Ohio	(216) 381-3320
Hollywood News	(301) 373-5965
Twilight Clone	(301) 946-8677
WorldNet	(301) 654-2554
Sleepy Hollow	(310) 859-9334
Hal 9000	(313) 663-4173
Tandy Harbor	(313) 455-3977
Charlie's	(314) 442-6023
St. Louis On-line	(314) 973-4073
Bytestream	(314) 657-1318
The Batboard	(314) 446-0475
Log On America	(401) 739-4100
HAWG WILD!	(402) 493-2737
Prime Time	(404) 667-0885
Shareware South	(404) 370-0736
NMC TBBS	(406) 265-4184
Infinite Space	(407) 856-0021
Bordertown	(410) 876-5101
Springfield Public Access	(413) 536-4365
EXEC-PC	(414) 789-4210
Blue Lake	(503) 656-9790
Advanced Systems	(503) 657-3359
Cajun Clickers	(504) 756-9658
Albuquerque ROS	(505) 296-3000
Software Creations	(508) 368-4137
Windows On-line	(510) 736-8343
Perfect Visions	(513) 233-7993
Digital Concepts	(602) 292-0065
Dark Shadows	(609) 627-8369
Other World	(615) 577-9342
Nashville Exchange	(615) 383-0727

Heart of Tennessee	(615) 890-8715
Microfone Infoservice	(908) 494-8666
24th Street Exchange	(916) 448-2483

E-mail

almanac@oes.orst.edu—Goofy mail server—send message "send quote" with subject blank to get back pithy saying—feeling down? send "send moral-support" instead, and get a pep-talk—then get a life

netaddress@info.cnri.reston.va.us—Knowbot directory service via e-mail—leave subject blank, send "query *<name>*" for search, "man" to have a manual sent to you

Anonymous FTP Sites

These sites were all still around when we went to press, but there's no telling when you'll be reading this, so nothing is guaranteed. They're in alphabetical order, with a brief description of what you'll find there after each. Those sites which we know have files leading you to other sites are marked with an asterisk, and the pathnames to the directories containing files listing more sites are given.

In the cases where we discovered you'll not be allowed anonymous access 24 hours a day we include the times you will be allowed in. Many if not all of these machines have day jobs and wish to preserve their CPU cycles for business during business hours. Times are assumed to be EST, but once again we remind you, nothing is guaranteed.

Since there is no guaranteed way to determine where a machine on the net is, we really should adopt GMT as a standard means of posting time, but no such plan is currently known to us.

achilles.doc.ic.ac.uk	*Location: /imported/categories
ames.arc.nasa.gov	Space memorabilia—9 p.m.-9 a.m.
atari.archive.umich.edu	Shakespeare from A to Z, well indexed
cocoa.contrib.de	*Locations: /t1/pub/doc/FAQ/... /t1/pub/unix/games/...
coe.montana.edu	History of TV—8 p.m.-8 a.m.
cs-ftp.bu.edu	*Location: /PC/AMIGA/Textfiles

cs.uwp.edu	Huge variety of music—7 p.m.-7 a.m.
elbereth.rutgers.edu	Science Fiction galore—6 p.m.-6 a.m.
faui43.informatik. **uni-erlangen.de**	*Location: /.home/amiga
ftp.cdrom.com	Mirror of **wuarchive.wustl.edu**
ftp.cerf.net	*Location: /pub/reze-2.rz.rwth-aachen. de/simtel/info-mac /report
ftp.cic.net	*Location: /pub/cicnet-*/...
ftp.cs.ruu.nl	*Location: /pub/NEWS.ANSWERS/ music
ftp.cs.tu-berlin.de	*Location: /pub/doc/music/lib
ftp.cs.widener.edu	TV files from *Trek* to *Simpsons*
ftp.eff.org	Internet, ethics and the law—24 hours
ftp.fu-berlin.de	*Locations: / /doc/faq/misc /doc/faq/usenet/sci
ftp.inf.tu-dresden.de	*Locations: /pub/doc/misc /pub/incoming/oberon
ftp.mathematik. **uni-ulm.de**	*Locations: /pub/info /pub/soft/oberon
ftp.netcom.com	Lists of FTP sites
ftp.nevada.edu	Guitar chords, photo news
ftp.nic.surfnet.nl	*Location: /mirror-archive/software/ info-mac/comm/info
ftp.pasteur.fr	*Location: /pub/FAQ/music
ftp.rrzn.uni-hannover.de	*Location: /ftp1/info-mac/comm/info
ftp.rz.uni-sb.de	*Location: /nfs/coli/pub2/ cs.tu-berlin.de/filelists
ftp.rz.uni-ulm.de	*Locations: /pub/VMS /pub/news-faq/...
ftp.switch.ch	*Location: /mirror/info-mac/comm/info
ftp.uni-paderborn.de	*Locations: /news/comp.archives/ auto/... /doc/FAQ/...
ftp.uni-passau.de	*Location: /mount/archive.theory/ answers/news.answers/music
ftp.uni-stuttgart.de	*Locations: /pub/doc/faq /pub/systems/...
ftp.uni-trier.de	*Location: /pub/info/faq/...

ftp.univ-lille1.fr	*Location: /pub/unix/faq/music
ftp.unt.edu	Libraries with on-line card catalogs
ftp.uu.net	Cornucopia (spend hours browsing)—24 hours
ftp.zam.kfa-juelich.de	*Location: /pub/ftp_info/ antivirus.ftp-sites.0894
ftp.zrz.tu-berlin.de	*Locations: /pub/languages/Oberon /pub/netinfo/internet
gatekeeper.dec.com	Recipes and such
harry.informatik. rwth-aachen.de	*Location: /pub/Linux/local/Docs
info.umd.edu	Clinton press releases etc.—6 p.m.-6 a.m.
lcs.mit.edu	Movie reviews—6 p.m.-6 a.m.
leginfo.public.ca.gov	California legal, bills, etc.—24 hours
mrcnext.cso.uiuc.edu	Books in electronic form—6 p.m.-9 a.m.
mrcnext.cso.uiuc.edu	*Classic literature on-line
ncsuvm.cc.ncsu.edu	Senate and Congress records—6 p.m.-6 a.m.
neeedc.umesbs.maine.edu	New England economics—6 p.m.-6 a.m.
nic.ddn.mil	Internet data and security info—6 p.m.-6 a.m.
nic.stolaf.edu	Travel advisories by country—7 p.m.-7 a.m.
nok.lcs.mit.edu	Hong Kong memorabilia—6 p.m.-6 a.m.
nptn.org	General Accounting Office reports—24 hours
nptn.org	Historical documents on-line—24 hours
nptn.org	Online classic literature—24 hours
pereiii.uji.es	*Location: /pub/mirror/mac/info-mac/ comm/info
pines.hsu.edu	Eskimo and Native American source
potemkin.cs.pdx.edu	Bob Dylan archive—9 p.m.-9 a.m.
ra.msstate.edu	Historical documents on-line—6 p.m.-6 a.m.
rs1.rrz.uni-koeln.de	*Location: /usenet/comp.archives/auto/...
rtfm.mit.edu	Pretty much everything—6 p.m.-6 a.m.

scitsc.wlv.ac.uk	*Locations: /pub/faq/music /pub/faq-by- newsgroup/rec
seq1.loc.gov	Plethora of Soviet documents—6 p.m.-6 a.m.
sumex-aim.stanford.edu	Macintosh shareware—9 p.m.-9 a.m.
town.hall.org	Annual reports and SEC data
uceng.uc.edu	*Location: /pub/wuarchive/systems/amiga/aminet/info/sites
whitehouse.gov	Position papers, transcripts, etc.—24 hours
world.std.com	Eclectic literature selection—6 p.m.-6 a.m.
wuarchive.wustl.edu	Cornucopia (spend hours browsing)—24 hours
zippy.nimh.nih.gov	*Location: /pub/reze-2.rz.rwth-aachen.de/simtel/info-mac/misc

Hardcopy Information Storage (Books)

For the most part, none of the items in this category require login ids or passwords. Some do, however, cost money. Those that are available on-line can be found with relative ease using any of the data harvesters discussed earlier.

Gofton, Peter W., *Mastering Serial Communications*,
California: 1986
Dvorak, John C., *Dvorak's Guide to PC Connectivity*,
New York: 1992
Stallings, William., *Data and Computer Communications*,
New York: 1985
Kochmer, Jonathan., *NorthWestNet User Services Internet Resource Guide*, Internet: 1991
Kehoe, Brendan P., *Zen and the Art of the Internet*, Internet: 1992
Electronic Frontier Foundation., *EFF's Guide to the Internet*, Internet: 1994

TELNET

access.uhcc.hawaii.edu	Bills before the Hawaiian legislature
access.usask.ca	Access to library catalog access heaven and hundreds of TELNET sites—type "hytelnet" at the login prompt
callcat.med.miami.edu	Database of AIDS health providers in southern Florida—login id: library
callsign.cs.buffalo.edu 2000	Ham radio directory with search capability
camms2.caos.kun.nl	Periodic table-indexed info database
cfa204.harvard.edu	Space cornucopia—login id: einline
debra.doc.ca	Databases with natural-language interfaces—login id: chat
envirolink.org	Environmental information—Login id: gopher
epaibm.rtpnc.epa.gov	Computerized card catalog of EPA documents
fdabbs.fda.gov	FDA database access system—login id: bbs
fedix.fie.com	Federal hiring database—login id: fedix
fedworld.gov	Federal information repository and system gateway—login id: new
forsythetn.stanford.edu	Martin Luther King data source—login id: socrates
ham.njit.edu 2000	Ham radio directory with search capability
hermes.merit.edu	Database of newspaper and magazine articles related to the environment—host id: mirlyn login id: meem
hpcvbbs.cv.hp.com	Info about Hewlett-Packard calculators
india.colorado.edu 13	Exact time according to the atomic clock in Boulder (in Mountain Standard Time)
info.cnri.reston.va.us 185	Knowbot information service—a directory search routine for the Internet
info.umd.edu	Already listed for FTP, also available for TELNET

internic.net	Access to the whois directory—who's who in the Internet
ipac.caltech.edu	Data on more than 100,000 objects outside the Milky Way—login id: ned
locis.loc.gov	Library of Congress information service
madlab.sprl.umich.edu 3000	Weather, ski, and hurricane forecasts
martini.eecs.umich.edu 3000	Geographic database
psupen.psu.edu	World weather and crop reports—login id: your 2-letter state code or WORLD
spacelink.msfc.nasa.gov	Space cornucopia
spacemet.phast.umass.edu	Space cornucopia—login id: your name

World Wide Web

Although we have made this a separate section, we will be listing FTP and TELNET sites here. Why? Because the WWW is not really a collection of places where you can find things. It is a collection of things that find the places for you.

Well, *that* was illuminating.

Okay, if you want to surf the web, what do you do?

You have two choices: TELNET to a site that has a browser available for public use and use that browser, or find a browser and load it on your machine. The latter choice is definitely preferable. Once you have a browser, you no longer worry about things like where to find stuff. You simply tell the browser what you're looking for and let it do the legwork for you. (There's an outdated piece of idiom for you.)

There are bunches of machines out there set up as web servers, and they will answer your browser's call for information if they have it. Many will also provide routing to other servers, which will answer if they have anything and route the request to still more servers, and so on, and so on.

At this point you see that the amount of information one of these browsers can return on a simple query is stupefying. This is where the real power of being interconnected with the world shows itself in all its resplendant glory. You'll get files, pictures, multi-media presentations, etc. A veritable plethora of information of every kind imaginable will come running to you at the click of a button.

Now that your interest is piqued, here are some browsers that are commonly available and where they can currently be found. Be forewarned, though. Like everything else on the net, anything in print is assumed to be out-of-date, and more and better browsers are being written as I am typing this. Greater interconnectivity, natural language query-processing, and eventually vocal-control front-ends are just around the corner. Luckily, with your not-quite-state-of-the-art browser, you'll be able to find out about all the new developments and where to get at them.

First, here are some places with browsers waiting for you to TELNET in and use them:

fserv.kfki.hu   login id: www—Hungary
info.cern.ch   no password required—Switzerland
info.funet.fi   login id: www—Finland
sun.uakom.cs no password required—Slovakia
vms.huji.ac.il login id: www—Jerusalem
www.njit.edu login id: www—New Jersey

As you can see, some of these sites are very far away, and the ones in Slovakia and Hungary don't run the fastest transport software. You are definitely better off going out and grabbing one that will work on your machine. The options you have are unfortunately limited in this regard. While there are several excellent browsers available for use on every machine imaginable, if you want the multi-media, the pictures, and the ease of use that's available, you'll need to upgrade your Internet access.

The problem is the nature of the connection you have to the machine serving as your gateway to the net. It's a window. One window. To take advantage of the power of the web, you need to somehow connect your entire display to the net, not just one window. You need some way to get your very own Internet address.

There are companies out there happy to oblige. It's not even in the neighborhood of cheap, but then you would really be on the net. Of course, you don't have to spend your entire salary on this. Amazingly enough, there is a way to get a temporary IP address each time you sign on to the net. In fact, there is more than one.

There are two commonly available ways to take advantage of all that the web has to offer from the comfort of your home. The first is called SLIP, which stands for Serial Line Interface Protocol. The second is called PPP, which stands for Point-to-Point Protocol.

Both SLIP and PPP establish a peer-to-peer connection between your machine and a gateway machine connected directly to the net. Your machine is assigned a temporary IP address for the duration of your connection. When you sign off, that address is freed for use by another surfer. Ask your local access company about these services. They cost a little more, but once you've seen the difference, you can never go back. DAPs usually offer them, FAPs not so often, and SAPs almost never.

Here then are some sites containing browsers freely available for downloading, along with the name of the browser, the directory in which you'll find it, and a description of the platform it runs on:

Sites	Browser Name	Directory	Platform
archive.cis.ohio-state.edu	w3browser-0.1.shar	/pub/w3browser	UNIX
ftp.cc.utexas.edu	url_get.tar.Z (batch)	/pub/zippy	UNIX (cron)
ftp.cs.unlv.edu	Chimera	/pub/chimera	X11/Athena
ftp.law.cornell.edu	Cello	/pub/LII/cello	MS Windows
ftp.ncsa.uiuc.edu	NCSA Mosaic for X	/Mosaic	X11/Motif
	NCSA Mosaic for VMS	/Mosaic	DECWindows
	Mosaic for Windows	/PC/Mosaic	MS Windows
	Mosaic for Macintosh	/Mac/Mosaic	Macintosh
ftp.omnigroup.com	OmniWeb	/pub/software	NeXTStep
ftp2.cc.ukans.edu	DosLynx	/pub/WWW/DosLynx	MSDOS
	Lynx	/pub/WWW/Lynx	UNIX
harbor.ecn.purdue.edu	tkWWW (Beta)	/tkwww<version>	UNIX/X11
info.cern.ch	Line Mode Browser	/pub/www/src	UNIX
	Samba ("mac")	/ftp/pub/www/bin	Macintosh

Sites	Browser Name	Directory	Platform
	WorldWideWeb	/pub/www/src	NeXTStep
max.physics.sunysb .edu	AMosaic	/pub/amosaic	Amiga
moose.cs.indiana.edu	w3.tar.Z or extras.tar.Z	pub/elisp/w3	emacs
ora.com	Viola for X (Beta)	/pub/www/viola	X11/Motif
	Viola for X (Beta)	/pub/www/viola	X11/Xlib
vms.huji.ac.il	For VMS	www/www_client	VMS

Whoa. No matter what machine, operating system, windowing system, of window manager software you have, you can get a browser that works with it. If you don't have time to mess with surfing the web, you can download a batch mode "browser" that runs while you're away. Satisfied yet? Huh?

PARTING IS SUCH SWEET SORROW

There it is. Even if 90 percent of the references in this section didn't lead you to more (which they do) you could spend years investigating them. This is just the tip of the iceberg, though. There is more out there than can fit in a thousand thousand-page books, and it's growing all the time.

The way we access information is changing, and inevitably, so is the way we think about it. Someone once said, "It's not important that you know something, as long as you know where to look it up." With the Internet well on its way to becoming the repository of all human knowledge, it won't be long before everyone knows where to look it up. Hopefully, now you know how to look it up, too.

Surf's up. See you in the datasphere.

Index